A PINK IMPACT RESOURCE

MAKE YOUR MARK

A 40-DAY DEVOTIONAL
FROM GATEWAY WOMEN

GATEWAY
PRESS

Make Your Mark: A 40-Day Devotional from Gateway Women
Copyright © 2017 by Gateway Publishing

ISBN: 978-1-945529-28-3 Paperback
ISBN: 978-1-945529-29-0 eBook
First Edition printed 2017

We hope you hear from the Holy Spirit and receive God's richest blessings from this book by Gateway Press. We want to provide the highest quality resources that take the messages, music, and media of Gateway Church to the world. For more information on other resources from Gateway Publishing, go to **gatewaypublishing.com**

Gateway Press, an imprint of Gateway Publishing
700 Blessed Way
Southlake, TX 76092

Table of Contents

PART ONE

Make Your Mark
at Home

Preface

As the Gateway Women's leadership team began to develop this devotional, we wanted to do more than share our own stories, revelations, or experiences. We wanted to introduce you to some of the most amazing and impactful women from our body who are making a mark in their own sphere of influence.

The following ladies have graciously allowed us to give you a glimpse into their hearts by sharing their personal stories. If you enjoy their contributions and want to stay in touch, speak to each other in one of the social media spaces.

- **Kassie Dulin** – A politically-savvy advocate who is standing up for biblical truth in the public arena.

  ▪ Kassie Dulin

  ▪ ▪ kassiedulin

  firstliberty.org

- **Erin Eisenrich** – An up-and-coming professional in the commercial insurance world who is an everyday evangelist.

  ▪ eeisenrich

- **Edra Hughes** – A grandmother to 20 who is using her legacy of faith and gifts of service to influence others.

  ▪ Edra Hughes

  ▪ edrahughes

- **Kristen Mangus** – A multi-talented entrepreneur who uses handmade crafts to engage a growing and vibrant online community.

  ▪ ▪ ▪ ▪ goodknitkisses

  goodknitkisses.com

- **Hala Saad** – An Egyptian-born media professional and humanitarian who is sharing the gospel in the Middle East.

  📺 tamamtv

  visioncommunications.org

- **Brooke Sailer** – An eighth-generation believer who teaches and uses hospitality in the home as a discipleship method.

  📘 This Thing Called Home

  📷 brooke_sailer

  brookesailer.com

- **Jessica Sheppard** – A worship leader, photographer, and fashion blogger who is influencing her generation through the creative arts.

  📘 jessicasheppardblog

  🐦 📷 jessicasheppard

  jessicasheppard.com

- **Amie Stockstill** – A powerful and engaging preacher and teacher who is investing in aspiring female leaders.

  amiehopestockstill

  amiestockstill

  Amie.tv

  amiestockstill.com

- **Wendy K. Walters** – An inspiring and motivating minister and business owner who is intentionally using her expertise in branding to help others express their passions.

  WendyKWaltersBiz

  WendyKWalters

  wendy.k.walters

  wendykwalters.com

- **Ebony Wright** – A wife, mom, author, and teacher who is helping single women prepare themselves for marriage.

  MarriagePLANS

  beforehefindsyou.com

We selected a cross-section of women who are using their interests and passions to serve others and bring honor to God. They aren't all professionals or formally-designated ministers. They are everyday women living everyday lives. Some are single, some married. Some are young and some are more mature. Some influence others from within their homes and some minister in the workplace. All of them use their gifts to encourage others and to share their blessings along the way.

As you get to know these women, we hope that you will recognize that you are just like them. It could be you featured in this book. Whatever your gifts or passions or stage of life, you can make a mark on people around you. Don't wait for what will be. Instead, begin *now*. God wants to use you in your everyday life to bless others. Let love be the platform on which you stand, and God will reveal those He has called you to impact.

Acknowledgments

Thanks to the Gateway Women's leadership team for their contributions to this devotional.

Hannah Etsebeth

Samantha Golden

Jan Greenwood

Lynda Grove

Sandy Jobe

Stephanie Kelsey

Dorothy Newton

Adana Wilson

Marsia Van Wormer

Lorena Valle

For more information about Gateway Women please visit

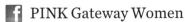 PINK Gateway Women

🐦 📷 gatewaypink

▶️ PINK Gateway Women

women.gatewaypeople.com

To learn more about Pink Impact Women's Conference please visit:

pinkimpact.com

You were born for impact.
He knows your name.
He knows your circumstances.
He knows your dreams.
You can make your mark.
You really, truly can.

What's Your Motivation?

Debbie Morris

You want your life to matter. You want to paint bold, beautiful strokes and small, intricate details that create a work of art. You want your life to be significant. You don't just want to plant a flower; you want to plant a garden of the finest flowers. You don't just want to write a letter; you want to write a bestseller. You don't want to buy a dress; you want to buy the mall.

Okay, maybe I am getting a little too excited about your potential with that last one; but you don't just want to survive, you want to thrive. You want to wake up each day excited! You want to live life to its fullest.

That is why motivation is so important. Motivation is often the difference between success and failure. It's the "why" behind the activity that makes all the difference. Knowing your "why" will guide your efforts.

There was a time when you were looking for rest, looking for something you couldn't describe, looking for hope. And then, in a desert, you found God looking for you. Look at the beauty of this truth in Jeremiah's words:

> They found grace out in the desert, these people who survived the killing. Israel, out looking for a place to rest, met God out looking for them! God told them, "I've never quit loving you and never will. Expect love, love, and more love" (Jeremiah 31:3 MSG).

The children of Israel were on what seemed like a confusing journey. God had intervened on their behalf. They had been slaves for as long as they could remember, but then God sent Moses to deliver them from the cruel hand of Pharaoh. God miraculously rescued them with incredible miracles, such as parting the Red Sea. But when they had an opportunity to worship the one true God, they returned to other gods. So God let them wander in the desert for forty years. True to Himself, God was also in the desert looking for them.

God wants a relationship with you in the same way that He did with the children of Israel. So what difference does this fact make in your own personal quest to Make Your Mark? You have to hear this:

If you have asked Jesus into your heart, you are accepted. Your quest to make a mark is not to find significance. You have significance. You are loved. You are highly favored. You are known by God. You are special.

Instead: motivation! Our motivation isn't to obtain love, favor, or good standing. We already have that. The motivation is love.

> "By this My Father is glorified, that you bear much fruit. As the Father loved Me, I also have loved you; abide in My love " (John 15:8–9 NKJV).

Everything we want to accomplish must be motivated by love—not by insecurity, and certainly not by fear.

In this devotional, we are going to offer you encouragement from God's Word so that you will be inspired in your pursuit to Make Your Mark. This is a collection of devotions from an amazing group of women; women just like you, who have fought insecurities, overcome obstacles, conquered fear, and built friendships with other like-minded women. This book will also introduce you to ten additional women who are making a real mark in their spheres of influence. They are a cross section of women also just like you; friends, singles, moms, leaders, business owners, and ministers. We are honored to highlight their faithfulness and recommend their stories to motivate you toward love. You are going to be blessed.

psdebbiemorris

God is within her.
She will not fall.

—Psalm 46:5 NIV

PART ONE
Make Your Mark at Home

People long for home. God created us with a desire to find and embrace a place where we feel safe and loved. In an ideal world, each of us grows up in a loving environment where we experience an abundance of peace and love. It's at home that we learn the most basic life skills and develop our most enduring character traits. We learn about who we are and where we come from.

If we pause to think about where we have the greatest influence, we will see that we make our mark at home first. The old saying "Home is where the heart is" contains much truth. We spend more time there than anywhere else. It's at home that we interact with the most significant people in our lives; it's at home that we give and receive nurture. We get up each morning soaked in the atmosphere we create. We launch our family and friends from within that atmosphere, then turn around and invite others right back into it.

We have a responsibility to guard the atmosphere of our homes. We have an anointing and an authority to live and love like Jesus within the four walls of our dwelling. Here we can shape, restore, and encourage our hearts by living according to the Spirit.

We don't long only for an earthly home or family. Even more, God created us to ache for our eternal dwelling. We find our true home in Christ alone; He has gone ahead to prepare a place for us.

As you begin this devotional, expand your understanding of home beyond the place where you live. Allow your meditations to take you to deep places of spiritual rest and trust, so that you might have strength and power to love others with great grace.

Day 1

The Proverbs 31 Woman

Samantha Golden

> She is clothed with strength and dignity,
> and she laughs without fear of the future.
> —Proverbs 31:25 NLT

I have always had a love/hate relationship with the Proverbs 31 woman. She's the woman I always wanted to be but felt like I could never become. My humanity always seemed to get in the way, or maybe it was my pride. Later, I found that I didn't fully understand who the Proverbs 31 woman is, what inspires her, or where her strength comes from.

The Proverbs 31 woman is clothed with strength and dignity and laughs without fear of the future. She is strong and steady. She is confident. She has self-worth. She is fearless. These are all characteristics I desperately wanted. I wanted to be confident. I wanted to be fearless. The question was, "How did she live this way?"

In Hebrew, the word for *strength* also means "boldness," "might," and "power." It includes strength of mind, heart, and soul. The Proverbs 31 woman lets God's opinion of her give her heart boldness, her mind power, and her soul might. The word for *dignity* also means "beauty," "majesty," "brilliance," or "splendor." The Proverbs 31 woman finds dignity and self-worth in what God says about her. She flourishes in God's promises.

I realized why I had been so frustrated with the Proverbs 31 woman: I had a wrong definition of strength and a wrong understanding of where dignity comes from. I had been living my entire life thinking that strength was something that I could muster up. If I tried hard enough, I could be strong. It meant not allowing my feelings to have a voice. To gain dignity, I learned to pretend that all was well and to make sure everything looked good. I was trying to prove my self-worth by thinking that if I did enough things right I would be OK. If I lost more weight or got a new look, then I would have value.

The Proverbs 31 woman connects with God from her heart. She is honest with her struggles and allows God to strengthen her spiritually, emotionally, and physically. She lets God define her worth and therefore she knows she has value. She walks in humility and confidence that is contagious. She serves those around her, both at home and in the marketplace, and people respect her for it. Because her strength and dignity come from the Lord, she can laugh without fear of the future. The storms of life don't move her because she knows the Lord is in control.

Make Your Mark

Is there a place in your heart that you need God to touch, heal, and strengthen? Do you want Him to clothe you in strength and dignity? Do you want to walk in boldness and confidence knowing that you are His and He is yours? He is just waiting for you to ask. Go ahead and ask Him now. He is faithful to answer. You will flourish when you live according to His promises.

A Legacy Marked by His Presence

Hannah Etsebeth

> Surely the Lord is in this place,
> and I was not aware of it.
> —Genesis 28:16 NIV

Many of us resonate with the feeling that no matter how grand our personal dreams, our hopes for our children run deeper and wider. They carry our legacy.

As a mom, I feel an urgency to pray for my children. However, because of that burden, I sometimes feel like there is so much I want to pray over them that I will never scratch the surface. It can be discouraging.

In Genesis, Jacob's father, Isaac, urged him to travel from Canaan to Paddan Aram to choose a wife from among the daughters of his uncle, Laban.

On the way to receive the promise of a wife, Jacob stopped to camp for the night. In a dream, an angel of the Lord came to visit him. Through that dream God gave Jacob a promise:

> Then God was right before him, saying, "I am God, the God of Abraham your father and the God of Isaac. I'm giving the ground on which you are sleeping to you and to your descendants. Your descendants will be as the dust of the Earth; they'll stretch from west to east and from north to south. All the families of the Earth will bless themselves in you and your descendants. Yes. I'll stay with you, I'll protect you wherever you go, and I'll bring you back to this very ground. I'll stick with you until I've done everything I promised you." Jacob woke up from his sleep. He said, "God is in this place—truly. And I didn't even know it!" (Genesis 28:13–16 MSG).

Jacob began the journey looking for the promise of a wife. But when the presence of the Lord came upon him, Jacob received the promise of his entire legacy. We share in that same legacy today through the life, death, and resurrection of Jesus Christ.

When you pray for your children, pray not only for the specific things that are on your heart but also for the presence of the Lord to come upon them. The presence of the Lord changes us, frees us, and strengthens our legacy.

Make Your Mark

What are you doing to experience the presence of the Lord in your home and in the places your children go? Write down some of the ways you can welcome the presence of the Lord into your home.

Day 3

Be Still

Sandy Jobe

Then they cried out to the Lord in their trouble,
and he brought them out of their distress.
He stilled the storm to a whisper;
the waves of the sea were hushed.
—Psalm 107:28–29 NIV

We live in a noisy, fast-paced world. Sometimes it's difficult to find a place to quiet our minds. Even then, a variety of interruptions bombard us, such as phone calls, crying kids, work demands, social media posts, and a never-ending internal to-do list. Has bedtime ever made you excited because you could finally get some peace, only to wake up at 3:00 a.m. with all the details racing through your mind again?

When we take on more responsibilities than we have time for, it makes our minds run after hours.

Even in the quietest room, it is hard to shut off our brains. When I am walking through stressful times, my mind never shuts down. Occasionally, the voice of anxiety becomes so loud that I hear it even when those around me stop talking.

During these times, three things help me block out the voice of the enemy so that I can hear the Lord's voice:

1. I have discovered that when I listen to worship music, God's presence fills my mind. When the presence of God comes, I find it easier to avoid the noise and distractions. Only the Lord's presence can quiet your heart. Only He can "still our storms to a whisper." We can only hear a whisper when we are quiet and totally focused on Him. Worship music helps me to gain that focus.

2. A quiet place before the Lord and away from the noise is a gift from God. Last year, my husband and I took some extended time away so that we could unwind and refresh. I learned something interesting about myself during

that time. It took me a few days to process my
heart and mind and finally get quiet; but, when
I did, fresh peace and vision for life began to
fill me. I came home with a new priority to find
those places of solitude in my life.

3. Obeying the Fourth Commandment – keeping
    a weekly Sabbath – helps create emotional
    (and physical) stillness to regain focus. Jesus
    reaffirmed that the principle of Sabbath
    still applies to believers. Take a regular time
    every week to get still and focus on the Lord—
    perhaps with some Sabbath traditions, such
    as preparing the Sabbath Challah bread. It will
    refresh and encourage you.

Commit yourself to the discipline of rest. Make
it a priority to let Him "still our storms to a
whisper."

Make Your Mark

Do you have a special place or time to meet
with the Lord? Experiment until you find the

rhythm that works for you. A little worship, some Scripture reading, a morning devotion, or just five minutes of quiet can really make a difference in your day. A weekly Sabbath celebration with your family will help bring order from chaos. Don't think of it as another thing on your list of things to do. The discipline of regular rest keeps everything else in perspective.

Day 4

Mother Mottos

Dorothy Newton

But those who trust in the Lord for help will find their
strength renewed. They will rise on wings like eagles;
they will run and not get weary;
they will walk and not grow weak.
—Isaiah 40:31 GNT

You can find thousands of books, blogs, and other instructional materials on the subject of parenting. It seems like everybody who is anybody has something to say on the topic.

I am no exception. While I can't claim credibility through any recognized degree, I gathered my confidence to talk about the issue of parenting, specifically single parenting, from personal experience.

The Lord has blessed me to be called "Mom" by two beautiful, well-adjusted young men. As a single parent, I don't believe for one second that their upbringing was all my doing. I recognize the influence of various teachers, friends, and mentors in their development. Having said that, I also know I have absolutely been the person who fed, hugged, pushed, and prayed my little family throughout life—every single day.

Looking back, I believe I can offer others encouragement and support by sharing three "Mother Mottos" that have had the greatest impact on my children:

First, strive to keep a positive approach in your home. As a parent, I quickly learned that my own attitudes and responses usually set the tone for the emotional environment. When my sons were toddlers, their daily routines included bumps and tumbles. I often had to resist the urge to cry with them when they fell, because when my kids sensed my distress, they would habitually launch into tearful tirades. However, if I stayed calm, they usually popped right up and moved merrily on their way. When I responded to each of their crises in a positive manner, it led to a better outcome, because they were taking their cues from me. I constantly pray that I can maintain self-control and keep a calm spirit with my kids, even today.

Second, prioritize your life. The clock doesn't care about our daily to-do lists. No matter how well we orchestrate our time, something will usually still be undone. I figured out early that it was too easy to park my children in front of the television or hand them an iPad as I attended to what I thought were top priorities. I had to decide to prioritize spending quality time with my kids. Sure, there were days when laundry didn't get folded, the floors were a bit grimy, and dust piles were in competition with the books on the shelf. Still, I accomplished my goal when I touched my children's faces and took the time to influence their minds and hearts. The apostle Paul says that we should focus on pure, noble, and praiseworthy things (Philippians 4:8). That attitude helps me prioritize activities.

Finally, learn to develop empathy and perspective. This last bit of advice was the hardest for me to put into practice. Practicing empathy meant that I had to do my best to put myself in my child's shoes. Perspective meant understanding how much maturity they should have according to their age. From this vantage point, I could see how it might be difficult to tell on another kid, explain an unexpected "D" in math, or "forget" to put dirty clothes in the laundry hamper. Patience and seeing from their perspective didn't necessarily change the outcome, including whether to discipline them, but the negotiation was heartfelt by both parties. Patience is part of the fruit of the Holy Spirit who lives in us.

As parents, we will never be perfect, but by intentionally making choices that show how we value and love our children we can make a significant impact on their future.

Make Your Mark

Have you thought about what your goals are as a parent? What attitudes and qualities do you want your children to develop? Pray, search the Scriptures, and ask the Holy Spirit to guide you into the priorities, practices, and perspective that will help you achieve those goals.

Day 5

Rejoice

Lynda Grove

Count it all joy when you fall into various trials,
knowing that the testing of your faith
produces patience.
—James 1:2–3 NKJV

In the middle of the pain and pressure of trials, this verse isn't always comforting to me. I am encouraged by knowing that my struggles will produce patience, but I don't necessarily feel like rejoicing.

No one likes to go through difficult times. Yet the New Testament encourages us to embrace trials and testing because God's Word promises that we will come out stronger, even victorious. The author of Hebrews tells us that all discipline seems painful, but that it later produces a harvest of righteousness and peace (Hebrews 12:11). The apostle Paul says that we are "trained" by it.

Leviticus describes a peace offering, which is a sacrifice of rejoicing, a celebration for what you need. It is an offering by fire – "a sweet aroma to the Lord." This offering was not mandatory; instead, people gave of their own choice. In this sacrifice, the fire consumed all the fat, but the meat was left for the person offering the sacrifice. The fat is the part that gives the meat its flavor and tenderness. That excess, the pleasantness and comfort, is stripped away and offered as a gift. The meat left from the offering was to be enjoyed in relationship with others (Leviticus 3:5). The Lord's presence was the only thing left to cling to in the end.

I receive blessing when I take my trial and offer it as a gift to the Lord. When I choose to rejoice in the middle of it, God receives it as something sweet, precious, and prized; He understands the nature of my sacrifice. I lay aside the pain and anguish that come from the testing and count them as an intimate, significant offering for Him.

I find deep comfort in knowing that He sees what I am going through, understands the intensity of the fire surrounding me, and, because I am dear to Him, He sees and receives my decision to rejoice. The experience also gives me the desire to go deeper and train myself—through the study of the Word and prayer—so that my spiritual roots grow deeper and I can better weather future trials.

Make Your Mark

When you face trials, you can rejoice knowing that a deeper relationship with the Lord will be your reward. Think about a trial you are now facing and then choose to make it a peace offering. Take a few moments and offer the Lord a sacrifice of praise. Allow God to consume the best of your gift and you will receive courage and strength, knowing that the meat of His presence is sufficient for all your needs.

Day 6

Mission Control

Adana Wilson

Trust God from the bottom of your heart;
don't try to figure out everything on your own.
Listen for God's voice in everything you do,
everywhere you go; he's the one who will keep you
on track. Don't assume that you know it all.
—Proverbs 3:5–6 MSG

You may not struggle with control, but I do. My personality likes to be in control. I am not a girl who loves changes in her life—not unless I have planned it on the calendar months in advance.

But I have come to realize that I can only control two things: my attitude and my actions. I can't control what others do or say, how my kids behave, what my boss thinks, what people in the world say, and I especially can't control what God does or doesn't do. I can only control my attitude and how I respond to a situation.

One of the hardest challenges we face in controlling our attitudes and actions is handling unmet expectations. We have expectations about all kinds of things, ranging from things as insignificant as the quality of our dinner or what we will get for Christmas to more important matters, such as our relationships, success at work, or how others should treat us.

About five years ago, my husband and I were discussing plans for our wedding anniversary. After much consideration about finances, kids' schedules, and work schedules, we decided to invest in a night away at a local hotel. We had not spent the night away in a hotel for three years and I developed high expectations for the trip.

Sadly, however, the trip was a disaster from the beginning. It seemed like everywhere we turned something unexpected happened. The hotel added fees we were unaware of until we arrived. The high-end restaurant we planned to eat at ended up being closed for a private party; we waited almost two hours at another restaurant, which caused us to miss the movie we had planned to see. Then at 2:00 a.m. the pipes in our bathroom began to sound like a jackhammer was rattling them. After three calls to the front desk, one visit from a maintenance worker, and two hours later, the hotel finally offered to move us to another room. We opted to leave instead.

Talk about unmet expectations!

So what's a girl to do when all that she planned, expected, and hoped for doesn't happen the way she wants it to? We can either become disappointed, frustrated, and angry, or we can control our attitudes and actions. How do you do that?

First, be honest with the Lord and share with him your disappointments, frustrations, and questions. You can say things like, "I didn't like the way this happened," or "That situation hurt me." The Psalms are full of honest emotions and questions from King David and others. David was a man who God said was "after His own heart." And David was honest with God.

Second, choose to trust God's nature. You can trust God because He loves you unconditionally and wants the very best for you. When you know God and trust His heart toward you, you can more easily overcome your disappointments and rebound from your frustrations.

Finally, listen for and release yourself to follow God's plans. Jeremiah 29:11 says that the Lord has plans for you, plans for a hope and a future that will prosper and not harm you. These are God's expectations, not your own. When you don't allow missed opportunities, disappointing events, setbacks, or other unmet expectations to control your life, you gain victory and the Holy Spirit will fill you with joy and peace.

Make Your Mark

What unmet expectations are you dealing with today? Stop a moment and voice those to the Lord—remember He loves you and wants you to be honest with Him. Let go of any negative attitudes. Trust God and choose to leave those unmet expectations with Him. Lastly, ask the Holy Spirit to reveal God's plans for you. He is a good God and will fill you with joy and peace.

Day 7

All Your Children

Samantha Golden

All your children will be taught by the LORD,
and great will be their peace.
—Isaiah 54:13 NIV

Motherhood has given me my greatest joys and my greatest pains. At seventeen years of age and still a child myself, I wasn't prepared for all the ups and downs of motherhood. It wasn't easy, and I let fear drive me and steal my peace and, at times, my sanity.

When my girls were young, I was in a life group with a very wise woman who spoke truth to me. She told me that life and death were in the tongue and I had a choice—trust God with my daughters or continue to let fear drive me and overshadow the precious moments I had with them. She reminded me of God's promise in Isaiah 54:13.

I needed to believe that the same God who was teaching and leading me was the God who would teach and lead my daughters. Motherhood wasn't about micromanaging their lives, but about trusting God and getting a word from the Lord about who He created them to be. So I started helping my daughters make a God-given declaration over their lives.

Every morning, before they could get out of the car, I would lead them to say, *"I am a mighty woman of God with a calling and destiny on my life that I will fulfill. I am the head and not the tail. I am above and not beneath. I am blessed going in and blessed going out."*

As my daughters grew, there were times they did not make the best decisions and I had to fight fear and my desire to control. I had to remember that the Lord would also teach my children. He was active in their lives. I would remind my daughters of that declaration they spoke over themselves so many times. Today, my girls are young women and each has a personal passion to love and serve God.

Raising children is not for the faint of heart, but learning to stand on the promises of God will sustain you in the most difficult times and help you shape your children's future.

Make Your Mark

Have you opened the Word of God and found a promise for your children? Jeremiah 29 says that the Lord has plans for them. As a mom, you have a unique and powerful influence on the lives of your children. Take time to develop a list of biblical promises and make your own declaration for your children. Begin right now to declare over your children the plans God has for them. Then teach them to declare God's promises for themselves.

Day 8

Remembering the Good Times

Sandy Jobe

But the Helper, the Holy Spirit, whom the Father will
send in My name, He will teach you all things, and
bring to your remembrance all things that I said to you.
—John 14:26 NKJV

There is a great deal of teaching available today about how to be healed from the hurtful memories of the past. These teachings are helpful and valid. I personally have needed healing from hurtful memories. However, equally important are the good memories to help us walk through times of grief. Good memories are powerful tools to heal our lives.

If you have ever suffered the loss of a loved one, then you know the deep sense of grief that comes with their death. The deeper I have loved them, the deeper my grief. I have also noticed that in my most vulnerable moment, when the loss is consuming my thoughts, one small glimpse of a good memory can turn my tears into laughter. Then the joy of the relationship once again fills my heart.

My dad was a fun-loving, gentle giant of a man. Although he was tall in stature, he had a tender heart. I can still remember when he would correct me. Although he might have become upset, he would start his correction by saying, "Now shoog (short for sugar), you know that wasn't the best decision!" He was so kind. He loved life. As a little girl, I can still remember his laughter. He loved to laugh. He was also a generous man. I watched him bless those in need all the time. He loved to give. When I was on my honeymoon, the hotel manager called and said that someone had paid for another night if we would like to stay. I knew it was my dad. It was the little things that made him who he was.

In the days following his death, all the memories of my life with him came flooding back. Although those memories made me miss him even more, they also began to bring gratitude into my heart. I am a better person for having known him. Sometimes I can still hear his voice and feel his influence in my life. My memories of him have helped me push through my grief.

Grieving a loss is the only way to heal from it. Pushing the memories or pain to the side only prolongs the process. So when the pain of your loss begins to smother you, ask the Holy Spirit to bring the good memories to your mind. Thank the Lord for the good times and let the power of those memories bring healing to your heart.

Make Your Mark

Thank the Lord for His blessings. Remember and cherish the good times, especially when you are in a time of grieving. If your good memories are few and far between, then today is a good day to make a new memory with those you love.

Introducing

Brooke Sailer

Brooke is a creative thinker, writer, artist, teacher, singer, and gift-giver. She is an eighth-generation Spirit-filled Christian who has a passion for home and family, which mean everything to her and her husband, Scott. Hospitality is the discipleship method they have chosen to demonstrate the love of Christ to others. She believes peace and love are the foundation of a healthy home and teaches women basic homemaking skills. Brooke is the author of *This Thing Called Home* and blogs at brooksailer.com. She is an inspiring young leader who embraces a family heritage of faith and uniquely blesses others with her passion and skills.

**How do you hope to make a mark
in the lives of others?**

Everyday problems and solutions for women at home have always fascinated me, especially those of stay-at-home moms. I want to empower and impact others at a deep level to help them solve their problems at home, stabilize their environment, and define a role or job description that fits their unique makeup and family. Why is this empowering and impactful? There's no difference between the miraculous and the mundane. God is in the details. Dishes. Laundry. Kids. Meals. Organization. Relationships. All of it. All of these are the work of the Lord.

How has your faith impacted your life?

My faith helps me shift from the problems we face to the solutions we create. I focus on problem-solving and logistics and teach basic skills. I believe these solutions are only possible by tapping into the unlimited resources that the Holy Spirit can provide. There is no success at home without believing in the impossible. Have faith that with God all things are possible. Know that He will empower you, because He lives in you, and He cannot fail.

What advice would you give to a woman who is concerned about whether her life is impactful?

Sometimes God doesn't call us to be great; He just calls us to be faithful. Your life can be impactful in the small, everyday opportunities when you choose to be faithful.

Do you have a guiding phrase you live by?

Most of the time "great" looks like faithful, faithful, faithful.

Fun Facts About Brooke

- She hoards gift-wrapping supplies.
- She loves chai tea.
- She took her four little kids on an extreme backpacking trip.

- She likes handwriting, musicals, and neutral colors.
- She is the owner of the curliest hair in the world.

Introducing

Ebony Wright

Ebony's beautifully, blended family includes five wonderful children and her husband, Michael. As the founder of Marriage PLANS, she has a passion to help single women prepare themselves for marriage. Ebony also authored *Before He Finds You: The Truth You Need Before You Meet Your Husband*, and a small group study, *Before He Finds You*. When she isn't volunteering, leading a small group, or ministering alongside her husband, you will find her dreaming about the upscale breakfast café she wants to open one day.

How do you hope to make a mark in the lives of others?

As a child, love stories mesmerized me, and I saw how my parents and other married couples interacted. At a young age I developed a passion for marriage. I knew it was something to be honored, but my road to marriage was a bit longer and more complicated than I had planned. A few failed relationships and one child later, I began to prepare myself in earnest for a successful marriage, even in the absence of a potential mate. I learned quite a bit as a single mother who came to know Christ just two years after becoming a mom. God has delivered me from addiction, self-sufficiency, and a broken family. I believe He has given me wisdom through my experiences and called me to encourage others who share my experiences. I want women to know God, walk in their purpose, and become whole and free. These foundations form a great marriage.

How has your faith impacted your life?

I want to live a life of transparency and help others avoid the mistakes I've made in life. I know that no matter what the circumstances look like today, with faith, God can transform any situation. I am still learning and growing in my own marriage, but I know it's not just so that I can be happy. It's so that I can help others walk in that same freedom. There is no sense in letting my mistakes go to waste. The lessons I learned are lessons to pay forward.

Do you have a key mentor who has made a mark in your life?

The first person that comes to mind is my oldest daughter's grandmother. Even though her son and I did not work out as a couple, she continues to be a positive influence in my life. It is because of her that I walk with Christ today. She prayed for me and invited me to church many times while I was pregnant. After I came to Christ, she discipled me, answering all the questions I had and some that I didn't. She mentored me on how to make a blended family work, which had a huge impact on how we do family today. She was transparent with me and told me not only what she did right, but also what went wrong. Her influence was big for me and I am forever grateful for her example.

Do you have a guiding phrase you live by?
The first time someone shows you who they are, believe them.

—Maya Angelou

Fun Facts About Ebony
- She wanted to be Wonder Woman as a kid. She's grown out of it since then. (She still thinks Wonder Woman is cool, though.)
- Her first career was in food and beverage, and she still calls herself a true foodie!
- She is married to a world-class Christian comedian. (Can you figure out who?)

PART TWO
Make Your Mark in the Marketplace

Have you ever considered the fact that Jesus was a small business owner? Or that many of his disciples were in a family business? Matthew worked for the government and Luke was a physician. Even Paul, who started out as a religious professional, became a tentmaker and had great influence in the marketplace.

You and I may be a little like the religious leaders of Jesus' day, believing that spiritual work is the responsibility of those called to full-time ministry. We tend to underestimate and devalue our spiritual influence and potential kingdom impact in our everyday work lives. How many of us excuse ourselves from "ministry" in our workplace because of this kind of thinking?

The Bible teaches us that those who are religious professionals are to prepare and encourage others in their own ministries. We should leave the assembly each week better equipped to minister in our homes and in the marketplace.

When you begin to consider your job as an assignment from God, your work life takes on a whole new dimension. You become a workplace evangelist, a marketplace pastor, or even an office prophet. When you become aware of your potential spiritual influence, you will view your coworkers with a different mindset. You will see them as people who have the most basic human needs of love and peace, which they can only truly receive from Jesus Christ.

While we are going about the business of business, we have a significant opportunity to represent Jesus in our everyday lives. These next devotions will help you develop a mindset of marketplace ministry and give you unique insights and opportunities to help you serve others while you work.

Day 9

A Season of Silence

Hannah Elsebeth

The one who calls you is faithful, and he will do it.
—1 Thessalonians 5:24 NIV

I always wanted to change the world. As a teenager, there were countless times I'd find myself on my knees asking God to use me to make a difference in the lives of people ... a lot of people. Following college, it seemed like He was answering that prayer. I was traveling, interacting with many "household name" celebrities, and seeing the gospel preached to stadiums of unbelievers. But then God had other plans—a move, a transition, a stock market crash—and I was serving at the drive-thru of a local coffee shop. That wasn't exactly what I had in mind when I decided to change the world, and God didn't seem to be explaining.

Many of us experience what I call a "season of silence," a time when no one seems to see us, when we lead nothing, and when we seem lost in silence. For those with dreams, big or small, a season of silence feels painful and lonely. There are many questions and often many tears. Even when I've seen a dream fulfilled, I find there is another hope, desire, or vision yet to become reality. Waiting faithfully amid the silence is difficult. For me, at the time, it was wondering why I was serving lattes. How could I possibly make a difference in that place?

I wonder if David sometimes felt that way when he was tending sheep. Did he have any idea that there were bigger dreams in store for him? Before Samuel prophesied over him, would he have despaired of ever progressing beyond being a lowly shepherd—no less someday becoming king? And as we see in some of David's psalms, even when he served as king there were many times when he questioned whether he was in the right position.

I'm certain Joseph felt that way in the silence of the pit and the loneliness of the jail cell before his dreams became reality. Both David and Joseph used their seasons of silence to develop their trust in God and, thus, they changed their world.

The apostle Peter says:

> So be content with who you are, and don't put on airs. God's strong hand is on you; he'll promote you at the right time. Live carefree before God; he is most careful with you (1 Peter 5:6–7 MSG).

I now realize the potential we possess to serve God powerfully in any circumstance, whether it be serving coffee or ruling a nation. I serve Him by serving the people around me, regardless of my circumstances. I am convinced that how well we trust God in our seasons of silence will determine the richness of our dreams fulfilled. If we can live carefree before God, we can trust Him to use us to change our world in whatever way He has called us. For me, for a season, it meant one steamy latte at a time.

Make Your Mark

Especially if you are in a season of silence, look around your workplace and consider why God has placed you there and how you can minister to those around you. Be specific and write down some of the actions you can take to demonstrate Jesus in your circumstance. Pray about them and then do them—you will be amazed at the fruit the Holy Spirit can bring.

Do Everything Well

Marsia Van Wormer

People were overwhelmed with amazement.
"He has done everything well," they said.
—Mark 7:37 NIV

The thought of doing something with *excellence* is daunting. You may think that you should do something brilliant or extravagant. You may compare your performance to things that others have done or to results that others have achieved. Comparison or fear of failure can cripple your thoughts and paralyze your actions before you have even begun. What if your best isn't good enough?

These thoughts can hinder you in the workplace as well as the home. What happens if that meeting does not go well? What happens if you don't meet the highest sales goals or get the best performance rating? What if your charity doesn't meet your donation goals? We usually know what our company or organization expects from us—but what does God expect?

God first expects excellence through obedience. Your performance will never achieve perfection. Rather, God values the highest use of your talents and gifts to further His purposes. When the apostle Paul talks about love in 1 Corinthians 13, he prefaces that chapter by calling it the "most excellent way" (1 Corinthians 12:31). Paul tells Timothy that those who serve well gain "an excellent standing" (1 Timothy 3:13). In Titus 3:8, Paul says that good works are "excellent and profitable for everyone." Nebuchadnezzar considered placing Daniel above his whole realm because of the "excellent spirit" that he saw in Daniel (Daniel 6:3).

In Colossians 3, Paul says that we should work at everything with all our hearts. God has uniquely gifted women in many ways, but often we are also put down because of long-standing discrimination. Don't be held back! You can achieve as much as you put your mind to—just don't let false expectations or unrealistic comparisons cripple your thoughts or paralyze your actions.

Excellence comes as the result of how you purpose to achieve that to which God has called you, by using the gifts and talents that He has given you, whether it be in your church, your home, or your workplace.

In Mark 7, Jesus obeyed the Father and acted with the power of the Holy Spirit, and the people saw that He had done things well—in fact, He had just performed miracles, such as restoring a man's hearing and speech.

When you trust and obey God and serve with the power of the Holy Spirit, you will achieve excellence in whatever you do—and you just might see a miracle or two performed as well.

Make Your Mark

Pray for opportunities to challenge yourself; to do something out of your comfort zone. Practice that skill, if necessary, and ask God to provide you with the ability to demonstrate excellence by doing all things well. Know that you are doing them for a judge and an audience of One—the King of Kings—and not for other people.

Day 11

Dig a Little Deeper

Jan Greenwood

> But whatever were gains to me I now consider loss
> for the sake of Christ. What is more, I consider
> everything a loss because of the surpassing worth of
> knowing Christ Jesus my Lord, for whose sake
> I have lost all things.
> —Philippians 3:7–8 NIV

This passage bubbles over with the apostle Paul's passion for His calling. He made a tremendous impact on the world over two decades of ministry. What made him tick? What drove him to carry out the work that he did? Paul was clear about his purpose and his passion.

Passion is an incredible motivator. It will drive you to do things you never thought possible. It will sustain you when you've yet to reach your goals.

It will give you the power to produce results—
kingdom results.

If I ask the typical woman what she is passionate
about, I usually get a version of the following three
responses:

1. "I don't know." (*Many people have never
   stopped to ask themselves what they are
   passionate about.*)
2. "I'm passionate about lots of things," followed
   by a litany of seemingly random possibilities.
   (*We are often indiscriminate in our passions,
   saying we love chocolate with the same
   measure of enthusiasm as we like our latest
   Netflix series, or sometimes even our spouse.*)
3. "I'm passionate about what I do." (*We tend to
   focus on what we do more than why we like to
   do it.*)

What we casually identify as passion is often just
an indicator of a root motivation we've yet to find.
Can you look beyond your activities and experiences and begin to discover things about yourself

you never knew? At Gateway Church, we use specific tools to help you identify your strengths and spiritual gifts. We also have a program to help you uncover God's goals and dreams for you and determine a path forward to serve Him in those areas.

Bravely digging around in the roots of your heart will launch you on a journey of self-discovery that can change everything. When you know the desires of your heart and can state them with confidence, and then pursue your dreams using the specific strengths and gifts God has given you, you will be able to accomplish more than you ever imagined.

Make Your Mark

The apostle Paul's great passion was to know Christ. What is yours? Do you have the motivation you need to accomplish something you've said you are passionate about? Do you know your strengths, talents, and gifts and how they can help you achieve your dreams? If not, consider finding out more about those areas of your life as well. Once you do, pray about how you can use them to be more of what God has called you to become.

Day 12

Taking Risk

Dorothy Newton

Trust in the Lord with all your heart
and lean not on your own understanding.
—Proverbs 3:5 NIV

A job is just a job, or is it? And does it have to be? These are the questions I asked myself when my career path hit a dead end with a resounding thud. My crossroads moment came suddenly, as I realized there was absolutely no way I could get another promotion in my field, no matter how hard I worked. I needed additional education, but the last thing I wanted to do was go back to school. Just the idea was paralyzing. I had too many responsibilities in my daily life. It was too hard—too much. It wasn't until I connected with a childhood memory that I began to think differently.

My childhood experience is likely familiar to you. Remember the first time you rode a bicycle. Were you excited? Of course you were! Did you manage to ride the bike very far the first time? Probably not. Chances are, like me, you had your share of skinned knees and bruised elbows.

Now, fast forward to today. What comes to mind when you think of riding that same bicycle? You may remember the wind blowing through your hair or the group rides you made with your friends to get a soda or candy. My point is that few of us daydream about the crashes we made on the concrete. I vividly recall flying down unpaved neighborhood roads, arms high in the air, exhilarated by my own daredevil performance. Tears and Band-Aid moments from those days are dim and vague.

Just like learning to ride my bike, returning to college for my MBA turned out to be both bumpy and fun. More than my grades, I battled with daunting insecurities as to whether there would be enough time, money, and energy to accomplish my goals. I also lived in a state of uncertainty whether there would be positions available when I graduated that would make enduring the experience worth the effort.

Eventually, I completed my degree. Going back to school opened career doors that otherwise would not have been possible. I realized then how important it is not to get mired down in your current circumstances. In almost every career situation, there are options; upgrading your education, moving to another company, or even starting over in a new field.

I'm grateful I took the risk. I am thankful I pressed on during the bad days. Paul speaks of pressing on toward the goal in Philippians 3:12. Today, I can honestly say it was well worth the ride.

As you contemplate new prospects there will be a host of emotional battles. If you don't fight them head on, then you risk never fulfilling your potential. You need to develop a tolerance for greater risk. After all, a job doesn't have to be *just a job*. It can be the place where your passion lives. It can be a place for learning and growth and thereby a stepping-stone to a greater vision. It will definitely be a place where God has called you to serve and glorify Him in new ways.

Make Your Mark

Are you considering the limitations of your current position? Are you dreaming of a job that is more fulfilling or rewarding? If so, seek God for a vision for your future and ask Him what must be done to move in that direction. Once you have made the decision to move ahead, don't give up. Go ahead and take off those training wheels and discover the joy of riding into a new season.

Day 13

Fully Alive

Samantha Golden

You're familiar with the old written law, "Love your friend," and its unwritten companion, "Hate your enemy." I'm challenging that. I'm telling you to love your enemies. Let them bring out the best in you, not the worst. When someone gives you a hard time, respond with the energies of prayer, for then you are working out of your true selves, your God-created selves. This is what God does. He gives his best— the sun to warm and the rain to nourish—to everyone, regardless: the good and bad, the nice and nasty.
—Matthew 5:43–46 MSG

I believe we all have a gnawing feeling from time to time that we aren't living as "fully alive," or out of our whole heart. Something inside of us screams, "There's more!"

To live from the heart takes courage. It sounds so easy in theory, but is quite difficult to live out. Our human nature is to self-protect and figure out the safest way to make it through life without getting hurt. But if we are going to live the full life that Christ came to give us, we must live from the heart. John Eldredge says, "The glory of God is man with his heart fully alive."

To live from the heart takes risk: a risk to love, a risk to stand up for someone, a risk to believe in someone, a risk to enter into someone else's pain. Love is risky. Christ never asked us to only love those who love us back.

As followers of Christ, we are to bring life everywhere we go. It's love that frees those around us, not judgment. It's love that tears walls down.

When Martin Luther King Jr. got involved with the Civil Rights movement he wanted to create a peaceful revolution. Many people told him that would never work. When radical white supremacists bombed Dr. King's home, he was at home with his wife and young daughter. The blast ripped through their house, tearing off its entire front, narrowly missing his family. Within minutes, angry black militants arrived. They tried to convince Dr. King to fight back with violence. But Dr. King stood on the rubble of his front porch and proclaimed forgiveness for the perpetrators. Dr. King knew he could not fight hate with hate. He had to fight hate with love. Our nation is a better place because of Dr. King and his refusal to hate when it would have been so easy to return evil for evil. He believed that he could make a difference and when tested, he refused to give in.

If we, God's children, were determined to love and make a difference and woke up each day resolute to bring the kingdom of Heaven to earth, our world would be a better place.

Make Your Mark

Ask the Lord to show you how to love those in your life who have hurt you. Ask the Lord to let you see them through His eyes. Choose today to live with a heart fully alive, one that restores others, believes the best, and brings out the good in everyone you encounter.

Anointed for Business

Hannah Elsebeth

But in your hearts revere Christ as Lord.
Always be prepared to give an answer to everyone
who asks you to give the reason for the hope that
you have. But do this with gentleness and respect.
—1 Peter 3:15 NIV

P aul was a tentmaker. Luke was a physician.
Peter and Andrew were fishermen. In fact, if
you consider the lives of the twelve disciples, you'll
soon see that they were all working in the marketplace. It's our tendency to think of those "making a
difference in the kingdom" as only those in full time
"ministry." Nothing could be further from the truth.

When I was a teenager, I always thought that
the people who did the really great things for God
were the ones who had a title of pastor, missionary,

or evangelist. But as I found myself smack dab in the middle of corporate America, I realized my greatest mission field at that moment wasn't on foreign soil, but it was right there in the office. When I began to see people in our office coming to faith in Christ, that's when I really began to see how uncomplicated the Great Commission was. I found that being true to myself was the most natural thing; being prepared to answer, with gentleness and respect, those who asked me the reason for the hope I have. When people ask questions of substance, it's enough to just be honest, rather than being politically correct and dancing around the faith questions someone is asking.

In your marketplace, you can minister to others and see them saved, set free, and healed. The question you must ask yourself is, "Am I willing?" Are you willing to minister courageously in your employment? Are you willing to treat your workplace like a mission field?

Make Your Mark

Write down three actions that you can take to minister in your job. Pray over those things and consider who God has called you to encourage. Then be bold and reach out with gentleness and respect. Take a step or two to demonstrate the love of Christ to those in your workplace.

Day 15

Everyday Wisdom at Work

Lynda Grove

Jesus increased in wisdom and stature,
and in favor with God and man.
—Luke 2:52 NIV

J esus spent most His life doing just what you
and I do. He woke every morning to face the
routines of the day. Like many of us, he got up and
went to work. We rarely think about it, but He was
a businessman, working as a carpenter. He must
have faced mundane routines and the complica-
tions that come from relationships.

I like to imagine Jesus in His workplace. I wonder
if customers would stop in for routine business
transactions only to feel the warmth of His love and
experience a change in atmosphere. Maybe Joseph
arrived at the shop to find his colleagues fascinated

by his Son. Did they linger over small talk of wood and nails just to be near Him?

My husband and I married shortly after I graduated from Texas A&M University. He had some schooling left to finish, and we settled into our first home together in College Station, Texas. As you can imagine, the job market in a college town is bursting with applicants. After trying to find a job that fit my major, I decided to take a temporary job as the technical assistant to a team of engineers.

After the newness wore off, I found myself struggling with the boring routine of my duties in a negative environment where complaining and disparaging comments about management abounded. One morning during my time with the Lord, He helped me realize that I had begun to adopt the same attitudes, and He challenged me to bring His kindness, love, and hope into the situation. I learned to do my part through doing simple acts of kindness, keeping a positive attitude, and refusing to listen to the grumblings of my coworkers. Soon I found myself counseling and encouraging others. Even the engineers I worked for began complimenting my contribution to the office and rewarded me with a promotion.

My coworkers thanked me for brightening their work day and for the influence I was having in their personal lives. I was taken by surprise. I was enjoying meeting my challenge. Suddenly the mundane routines had become fulfilling, though it didn't seem to me that I was doing anything extraordinary. I prayed daily that the Lord would use me to bless others and give me wisdom as I faced challenging conversations, but I was simply finding practical ways to love and bless others.

Luke 2:52 tells us that as Jesus grew up, He also grew in wisdom and stature and in favor with God and man. We can find comfort knowing that He can relate to our everyday life and that, if we ask, He will cause us to also grow in wisdom and favor. Our workplace can be an opportunity for others to feel the warmth of His love and a change in the atmosphere.

Make Your Mark

Ask God to increase your wisdom and stature in your workplace. Pray about your place of employment and your coworkers and how you can bless them. Invite the Lord into your workplace and extend His love to everyone you encounter.

Introducing

Erin Eisenrich

Erin is an up-and-coming, young commercial insurance professional. She is a highly motivated, single working woman who is unafraid to set big goals or to pursue big dreams for herself and others. In a world where many women find it easy to imitate others, Erin is a fresh face of grace, living as an incredible example by being the best and most unique version of herself. She is unapologetically fashionable and a community-minded influencer. Most importantly, Erin is passionate about her love walk with Jesus.

How do you hope to make a mark in the lives of others?

When I was growing up, I so badly wanted to be a missionary and go overseas. I would ask God to give me the gift of evangelism, so that I could tell people about Him all the time. Instead, God sent me into a cubicle at a Fortune 500 company and gave me the gift of intercessory prayer. Just this morning God gave me a picture of how my job is like a house and everything else in my life is the stuff that happens in and around the house. It is not the house (job) that matters, it is everything that happens in and around the house that is significant. My job is a framework that gives me opportunities to influence people. When I started working in the corporate world, I would never have dreamed that such conversations would become an integral part of my day-to-day life. It is amazing what God can do in the small and unseen places.

How has your faith impacted your life?

My name, Erin, means *peace*. I do not know if my parents chose that name because of its meaning or if it was a happy coincidence, but I do feel strongly that the Lord named me Peace and gave me a mantle of peace and a gift of intercession. My hope is that being around me would encourage other women to find peace about a specific moment or circumstance in their lives—and for life in general—and that I would bless them through intercessory prayer. We are all going to have struggles and unmet hopes, dreams, and desires. I believe that the peace of the Lord and our opportunity to partner with Him in prayer can be a source of hope and inspiration in any season of life.

Do you have a key mentor who has made a mark in your life?

My mom once told me that I collect mentors. It's true. The Lord has blessed me with many great mentors and role models. My mom and grandmother would certainly be near the top of that list, but my grandfather stands out as the single greatest influencer on my life. We called him Papaw, and he loved me so unconditionally. He was always going out of his way to do sweet things for me simply because

I was *his* granddaughter. He was one of the most generous and faithful people I know, though I did not fully realize it until after his death: People came out of the woodwork to tell us things that he had done for them over the years. His love and generosity left a legacy for our family that will last for a long time.

Do you have a guiding phrase you live by?

Whether you turn to the right or to the left,
your ears will hear a voice behind you saying
"This is the way; walk in it."

—Isaiah 30:21 NIV

Fun Facts About Erin

- She is a girly-girl inside and out, but she also likes to hunt and shoot.
- She is available for blind dates most Mondays through Thursdays.
- She is actively involved with Dallas CASA (Court Appointed Special Advocates) on behalf of children now being cared for through the Texas Department of Family Protective Services.

Introducing

Kristen Mangus

Kristen is a multi-talented entrepreneur with a heart as big as Texas. She is the owner, host, and creative director of *GoodKnit Kisses*. *GoodKnit Kisses* is a company positioned to inspire, encourage, and empower people through education and design. She's built a large and loyal online community of followers by sharing her personal passion for knitting and all things creative through YouTube video tutorials, Facebook live broadcasts, blogs, and patterns. Her vision is to leave an inspired crafting world for future generations that continues to teach and reach others. She and her husband, John, have three amazing kids.

How do you hope to make a mark in the lives of others?

I love to encourage women to find their passion. Such joy arises when we find the "thing" our Maker created us to create. I encourage others to seek out the things that they enjoy creating, teach them to expand their skills and knowledge, and then inspire them to use that thing to bless others. In this way, we all can become the hands and feet of Jesus. What better way to show love than to create things, actually with stitches of love, and then give them away with love and a hug?

How has your faith impacted your life?

My work happens to be in the spotlight, so whatever I do is open for others to see. My faith helps me to respond with love and encouragement through social media. I let people who follow me know what I do and why I'm passionate. When prompted, I share pieces of my story, including a history of child abuse, a significant head injury that affected my memory, and my struggles with post-partum depression. God has grown my sphere of influence and my ability to influence others as I honestly share about my own journey.

What advice would you give to another woman who is concerned about whether her life is impactful?

Ask God for a creative idea and then follow it through. There was a season in my life when I felt something significant was missing. I talked to the Lord and He simply said, "You're missing your 'crafty.'" Boom! That was it. *GoodKnit Kisses* was born. Even though I was in a highly creative job, there was something about working with my hands that especially satisfied me. I began making tutorials on my own YouTube channel and grew to lead a small group to share my love of knitting. Today I work with women worldwide, encouraging them to make their own handmade gifts and share with other women. God will take the smallest obedience and use it to bless others.

Do you have a guiding phrase you live by?

A smile is a curve that sets everything straight.

Fun Facts About Kristen

- She loves to sing, be silly, and be a part of musical theatre.
- She survived a significant head injury twenty years ago and began making videos to help her short-term memory.
- Her first career was as a professional interior designer.

Choose kindness
and laugh often.

PART THREE
Make Your Mark as a Leader

Leadership skills matter throughout your life. Whether you are the head of your household or president of a nation, being a good leader is critical to success. There are many resources available to help you grow your skillset as a workplace leader, yet we often lack education and inspiration about the importance of becoming a *spiritual leader*.

When Christ becomes the bedrock of your life, you immediately become a different kind of influencer; a different kind of leader. Each of us has a particular set of strengths, gifts, and a calling that uniquely equips us for impacting others in a positive manner.

It's important that your leadership mindset is based on a strong spiritual foundation that will help you lead and influence others in every season and assignment of your life. This foundation helps you develop a healthy attitude and standard as a godly woman that's based upon the Word of God and not upon your own personal experience or opinion.

The following devotions are not about how to improve your productivity, maximize your marketing, or increase your profit margin. Rather, you will be inspired to look beyond the obvious or common to discover and embrace what drives you and makes you qualified to be a leader. We are coaching your heart toward a right alignment with the Holy Spirit that helps you identify your spiritual gifts and learn how to use them to lead others. Then you can embrace a life of strength, service, and courage based on love and mutual respect for others.

Busy, Busy, Busy

Stephanie Kelsey

Real wisdom, God's wisdom, begins with a holy life
and is characterized by getting along with others.
It is gentle and reasonable, overflowing with mercy
and blessings, not hot one day and cold the next,
not two-faced. You can develop a healthy, robust
community that lives right with God and enjoy its
results *only* if you do the hard work of getting along
with each other, treating each other
with dignity and honor.
—James 3:17–18 MSG

I've been struggling with answering the question
"How are you?" Often I say, "Busy," even though
I don't particularly like this response. I wonder
how my answer makes the other person feel. Does
she feel like I don't really have time for her? Does

she feel sorry for me? Does she wonder if I am brushing her off?

I am in leadership with many women and I often hear them say to me, "I know you are really busy, but …" as if they are apologizing for taking my precious time. Ugh! The last thing I want anyone to think is that they are a burden or I am "too busy," especially people I love and feel honored to serve. The same applies in my home. How often have I told my husband or children that I was too busy for something?

Being a servant leader requires time. I can't think of many situations where Jesus "brushed off" someone asking for help. I asked the Lord for guidance on how to respond to my family, friends, and colleagues when they ask how I am doing.

Often when I start a conversation with God, I feel as if He has been patiently waiting to talk with me. Sometimes it takes months for me to weed through all my excuses for why I run my life the way I do before I am finally ready to listen and receive the guidance of the Holy Spirit. In this case, however, the answer came quickly.

The Lord reminded me of His own words:

> "Whoever wants to become great among you must be your servant, and whoever wants to be first must be your slave—just as the Son of Man did not come to be served, but to serve, and to give his life as a ransom for many (Matthew 20:26–28 NIV).

Jesus dramatically modeled this kind of leadership when He washed His disciples' feet in the upper room. This act of service took precious time that He could have used to tell His disciples other, more practical things while the Roman soldiers were coming to arrest Him.

The apostle Paul also reminds us that the purpose of servant leadership is to prepare the church for works of service and build up the body of Christ (Ephesians 4:12). That is the reason God has given you gifts and talents to use as a leader, whether in your family, the church, or the workplace.

So what do I say now when someone asks me how I am doing? "I have a lot going on and I love what I'm doing. How can I serve you?"

Make Your Mark

Do you sometimes seem too busy for others? If you are too busy to serve, then you are too busy to lead. Ask God how you should respond to people when they approach you for advice or help. Treat every encounter as an opportunity to wash someone else's feet.

Day 17

We Will Win!

Jan Greenwood

With God on our side we will win;
he will defeat our enemies.
—Psalm 108:13 GNT

This is the rally cry of my son's football team. This year they are being led by a new coach who is developing a mindset of victory. Following several years of heavy defeats and losing seasons, my son had begun to lose his love for the sport. When a new coach arrived on the scene, however, things began to shift.

My son went from "I'm not sure it's worth it" to shouts of "We will win!"

I've thought quite a bit about how that happened.

Coach spent some time getting to know the players before he revealed his strategy. He addressed their mindset first. They felt like losers. He began to declare they were winners. Then he set about conditioning their bodies for endurance. He aligned them as a team in positions of strength. He made them push themselves beyond their previous limits, and then he surrounded them with words of courage and shouts of victory.

At first, when my son shared the rally cry, he kind of shrugged his shoulders. He thought the rally cry was a little overly optimistic. Nevertheless, he's a leader—so he shouted "We will win!" among the loudest, demonstrating his willingness to try. Slowly, day by day and practice by practice, he began to believe.

We will win! We will win! We will win!

I am talking about football, but I hear a war cry of the Spirit.

Scripture tells us that we are in a battle with principalities and powers. The enemy, Satan, has many warriors on his side. The ultimate prize for that battle is not a football trophy—it is the souls of men and women.

Some days, the enemy gets the upper hand and we experience defeat. Just as we stretch out and take a step, it seems we stumble or fall. What seems within our reach sometimes slips from our fingers.

We must follow Christ who will release us from a mindset of defeat to one of victory. You can be confident in knowing that the ultimate outcome of this war we fight has already been determined. Christ has finished the work on the cross. He has disarmed darkness, taken back the keys to death and hell, and seated Himself at the right hand of the Father. *We will win—because He has won.*

Make Your Mark

Whether you enjoyed the thrill of victory or faced a setback of your own this week, commit to fight on with confidence. Put yourself through the paces. Address your mindset first. Begin by declaring, "We will win!" Then condition your heart for endurance. Position yourself in faith. Trust God and fight with courage and shouts of victory. Follow the example of the ultimate leader—Jesus Christ. Remember: He has already won.

Day 18

Birds of a Feather Flock Together

Lorena Valle

And let us consider how we may spur one another
on toward love and good deeds, not giving up meeting
together, as some are in the habit of doing,
but encouraging one another—and all the more
as you see the Day approaching.
—Hebrews 10:24–25 NIV

The end of the year has always been special for me. Sunsets change, temperatures start cooling down, and freshness fills the air. At the same time, I start noticing large groups of birds migrating toward warmer weather. If you stop at a red light, the powerlines are full of birds that are taking a break from their journey south. I often see them flying in a classic "V" pattern called *flocking*.

Flocking enables birds to fly farther using less energy because when the strong leader flaps its wings, it creates uplift for the birds behind. Each following bird flies in the upwash from the wings of the bird in front. This enables the flock to use less energy and reduces fatigue.

God has called us to follow Him for the long run; not just a season, but for a lifetime of influence and service. We need to learn how to best use our gifts and energy to lead well. As I grew older I came to realize how important it is to be in a "flock," especially when the going gets tough. Being part of a community has helped me gain wisdom about how to grow strong as a leader. Here are four principles you can put into practice yourself:

1. *Don't fly alone.* Stick close to the women in your life who encourage you to grow in the knowledge of Christ. You will find protection in the flock.

2. *Rest.* When birds flock, they continuously change direction—each time this happens, a new leader emerges and the previous leader

rests and follows. When you fly with a group of women, you will rely on each other's strengths to lead at different times and in various circumstances. Remember, it is about building His kingdom.

3. *Be an encourager.* Sometimes geese at the back of their flock will make honking sounds to encourage the birds ahead to maintain their speed. Be willing to serve those around you by taking a place in the pack that might not be as glamorous, but it is as important to the team as being in front.

4. *Stay flexible.* Has your life been a straight line to where you are today? Or does your life look more like your path has shifted and taken you places you didn't know you would go? Oh, how many times I wished that God would give me turn-by-turn directions, just like a GPS—but I gain much more by joining Him for the ride. It is a joy when He leads me!

Make Your Mark

Are you investing in a local community of women or are you flying solo? When you "flock" together, it fosters health and safety for you and others. Ask God to help you find ways to develop relationships, whether it be as part of a small group or making a new friend. When you do, look for opportunities to help others lead.

Day 19

Determined to Win

Dorothy Newton

Our heart has not turned back,
And our steps have not deviated from your way.
—Psalm 44:18 NASB

If asked to sum up my life experiences to date, I would probably divide them into two categories: those that contained successes and those that ended in failure. I would find incidents in my childhood, college days, and career. I would certainly place the birth of my two sons in the "win column" while adding a divorce under the "loss column."

Sometimes life just doesn't play out like we planned.

There's something to be said for taking the time to evaluate your personal history. Yet, you can skim over the most important part, the part where you hung in and endured, sometimes to the bitter end.

Within every task there is some level of adversity. Each time you conquer a difficulty, no matter how small, you gain the strength to take on bigger challenges. That inner strength can make or break you. If I look carefully, I can see the "win column" has just as many learnings as the "loss column."

In the end, it is determination that keeps you moving forward. You don't yet know how each life experience will end. How many people marry with the thought they will end up in divorce court? Conversely, how many runners can line up on the starting blocks at the Olympics, knowing they will take away a gold medal? Only determination can bring you to the end result—no matter how that eventually looks.

There are many experiences that won't end up on my list, because they never served a distinct purpose—win or lose. While I'm not one to live in the past, I still wonder about some of those things. If I had followed through with painting classes, where would my creations be today? If I'd gone on that mission trip back then, would I be traveling the world? Funny thing, though, the reasons you did not persist then may sound a bit hollow today.

As I reflect on this, I see my character toolbox has grown. I am more willing than ever to move with determination and face adversity. After all, I have a personal history to ground me. Dolly Parton expressed my sentiments exactly when she said, "The way I see it, if you want the rainbow, you gotta put up with the rain."

Make Your Mark

It can be hard to go back and revisit the ugly or difficult experiences. But often it is these very experiences that test and prove the strength of who you are. When you reflect on your past, do you see how the detours in life have been for the greater good or do you view them with regret? You learn from both your successes and your failures. None of it matters today because your joy is a choice, and it's new every morning, regardless of your current circumstances. What matters, as the Bible says in James 1, is that you persevere under trial. I am sure that was what inspired Abraham Lincoln when he said, "I am not concerned that you have fallen—I am concerned that you arise."

Day 20

Leading from the Heart

Adana Wilson

"Don't you understand yet?" Jesus asked. "Anything
you eat passes through the stomach and then goes into
the sewer. But the words you speak come from the
heart—that's what defiles you. For from the heart come
evil thoughts, murder, adultery, all sexual immorality,
theft, lying, and slander. These are what defile you.
Eating with unwashed hands will never defile you.
—Matthew 15:16–20 NLT

I want to ask you an important question: *How is
your heart?* Consider how you check most everything else in your life (food, sleep, exercise, behavior).
But do you regularly look at or evaluate your heart?

Many people think that everything starts with
our thoughts—that if we control our thoughts,
then that affects our words and actions. But the

truth is that those things are just a reflection of what is in your heart. Proverbs 4:23 (NLT) says, "Guard your heart above all else, for it determines the course of your life." Our heart governs our thoughts, words, and actions.

We know we can't live without a healthy physical heart. Likewise, to live and lead effectively as a believer you must have a healthy spiritual heart.

Your heart determines the course of your life. That is why your heart is so important to becoming a leader. People will follow leaders who are authentic and genuine in their actions. People will follow those who encourage and support others. People will follow those who make wise choices and fight with courage and conviction for what they know is right. Can you see the pattern here? In the wider world, leaders can rule and lead through raw power or personal charisma alone; but God has shown us a better way.

People will follow those who lead by serving others. Of course, Jesus was the perfect example of servant leadership. He devoted His entire ministry to leading people into truth and life. Servant leadership is leading from the heart—a heart that is in tune with God.

How do you get your heart in tune with God? The Psalmist says, "Behold, You desire truth in the innermost being, And in the hidden part [of my heart] You will make me know wisdom" (Psalm 51:6 AMP). Scripture says that God will give us wisdom, and Jesus Himself modeled how we should lead others by serving.

Becoming a servant leader isn't always easy, and you can become frustrated and discouraged if you don't always see yourself as effective. Don't worry. God knows, and He is there. You can't hide anything from God—nor does he want you to. When you are honest with Him, He will give you wisdom to guide your heart; and people will follow those who lead wisely!

Make Your Mark

Take time to do a heart check and ask God to examine your heart. Start by taking one heart characteristic that you can work on to become more like Jesus. Ask the Lord to give you wisdom to help you become a servant leader.

Day 21

God Allows U-turns

Sandy Jobe

> Behold, I will do a new thing,
> Now it shall spring forth;
> Shall you not know it?
> I will even make a road in the wilderness
> *And* rivers in the desert.
>
> —Isaiah 43:19 NKJV

I like road trips. I learned to read a map years ago. It was my job on road trips to navigate our journey. We carried an atlas that was about 24 × 18 inches in size. It was like taking a book of posters with us everywhere we traveled. There was a full page for every state, and some states had multiple pages.

Years later came MapQuest. We could go online, put in our starting point and the destination, and it would map out the trip for us. We printed each step and created a file folder full of 8 × 11 inch pages mapping out our entire trips.

Now we live in the world of GPS and smartphones. Most of the time, the GPS is a wonderful thing, but sometimes the system speaks a few seconds too late to turn and then a U-turn is needed. Many times, this scenario has become a point of contention between myself and my sweet husband. He often thinks the GPS might be wrong. As it gives a verbal command, "In 800 feet turn right," he immediately turns and blames the error on the GPS. One time when this happened, I said, "You are the athlete, pretend it's a football field. How far is 800 feet?" We laugh about it now. However, I should admit that it has been a tense subject on more than one occasion, especially when in traffic, or in an unfamiliar city, and when there is no time to take the scenic route. When you miss a command from the GPS, the voice says "at your nearest opportunity, make a U-turn," or if you veer away from the suggested route, the voice will say "return to the highlighted route."

Recently on a road trip, we were on a very busy street and, you guessed it, my sweet husband missed his turn. For the next mile, there were "No U-turn" signs posted at every intersection. Everywhere we thought would be a perfect place to turn around and get back on the original path was illegal.

The Lord used that situation to speak so clearly to me. I was reminded that He does not post "No U-turn" signs at every intersection. Quite the opposite. It is His heart that when we step out of bounds or get off the intended path, that we turn around. He calls it repentance.

Repentance is a good thing. It is in those times that He begins to nudge us ever so sweetly to turn around and return to the highlighted route that He has so clearly detailed in the Scriptures. In fact, sometimes we hear that still, small voice quickening our heart, saying, "This might be the wrong way!" That's when it is time to make a U-turn at the nearest opportunity.

Make Your Mark

Do you need to make a U-turn? Why are you afraid of turning around? What lies have you believed that prevent you from admitting that you're wrong? U-turn means a fresh start. It is a Do-Over. Ask the Lord for a fresh start today.

Day 22

The Spirit-Led Leader

Stephanie Kelsey

The unspiritual self, just as it is by nature, can't receive the gifts of God's Spirit. There's no capacity for them. They seem like so much silliness. Spirit can be known only by spirit—God's Spirit and our spirits in open communion. Spiritually alive, we have access to everything God's Spirit is doing, and can't be judged by unspiritual critics. Isaiah's question, "Is there anyone around who knows God's Spirit, anyone who knows what he is doing?" It has been answered: Christ knows, and we have Christ's Spirit.

—1 Corinthians 2:14–16 MSG

W*hy would anyone try to lead without the Spirit of God leading the way?*

I confess that I must ask myself this question often. When I am short-sighted and get caught up in being busy, distracted, impatient, and self-absorbed, I tend to focus on the physical things of life and not the spiritual.

The apostle Paul told the Corinthians that when they were spiritually alive, they would have access to all the Spirit is doing—all His power and potential for their lives. We are only able to receive the Spirit's gifts when we open our spirits to Him. Then the Spirit can give us power and change our hearts to be more like Jesus.

I have found that I am a more effective leader when I remain aware of these things:

1. I have access to everything God's Spirit is doing.
2. The Spirit of God wants to help and commune with me.
3. Jesus Christ has the answer to all things.

No matter what is going on around me, Christ knows, and I have Christ's Spirit in me. How powerful it is to know that the living God dwells in me: He knows all, He sees all, and He promises to give me wisdom and guidance when I ask for it. This is wonderful news! It helps me remember God's precious promise: "For those who are led by the Spirit of God are the children of God" (Romans 8:14 NIV).

Make Your Mark

Are you facing any issues or challenges that are holding you back from being an effective leader? Pray specifically and ask the Holy Spirit for guidance to use the gifts He has given you. Pray that you will be a Spirit-led leader.

Day 23

Leading at God's Pace

Adana Wilson

The Lord's plans stand firm forever;
his intentions can never be shaken.
—Psalm 33:11 NLT

I love to drive. I enjoy navigating through traffic and looking ahead to strategically assess which lane is moving the fastest so that I can get where I am going in the shortest amount of time. I have also been known, when traveling, to celebrate making it to my destination in record time.

I think many times we do that in our relationship with the Lord. Sometimes we look at a situation and try to figure out how to get the result we want as quickly as possible. We have a plan and may even start to manipulate things to make it happen. We can end up turning our preferences into what we think are God's promises when they are no such thing. This is especially dangerous when you are in a position of leadership—you will be dragging others along with you.

God just doesn't work that way. God wants us to understand that He is faithful and will provide according to His timing:

> "We do not want you to become lazy, but to imitate those who through faith and patience inherit what has been promised" (Hebrews 6:12 NIV).

Throughout the Israelites' wanderings, God taught them patience. The Scripture says, "The people grew impatient on the way" (Numbers 21:4 NIV). When they came to Canaan, they had to wait three days for the raging waters of the Jordan to subside. Why did God not bring them to Canaan in the winter, when the river would have been dry? Of course, even then, the ability to cross on that third day was a miracle— the harvest-time rains could have lasted for weeks. The Spirit was clearly not focused on getting results in the fastest way possible!

Our journey is no different. Patience is a fruit of the Spirit. Paul, James, Peter, and the writer of the book of Hebrews all talk of the gift of patience. I have yet to find a single instance where Jesus ran or hurried somewhere. Even when Paul talks about Christians running a race, it is a marathon rather than a sprint.

It is no surprise that even when I try to drive somewhere the fastest way, when the light turns red and I stop, everyone else catches up. I have wasted a great deal of time and energy, both for me and those who followed me. We live in power, joy, and peace when we decide to live by God's timetable and allow Him to set the pace.

Make Your Mark

Is there a situation in your life in which you are trying to make something happen at your pace instead of God's? Maybe you are frustrated or discouraged that things aren't working out as quickly or in the way you want them to. Submit those thoughts to God and ask Him for patience. If you are leading others on this journey, encourage them to trust God and His timing.

Day 24

Everything Speaks

Marsia Van Wormer

Love from the center of who you are; don't fake it.
Run for dear life from evil; hold on for dear life to good.
Be good friends who love deeply;
practice playing second fiddle.
—Romans 12:9–10 MSG

When my boys were about 6 or 7 years old, I would pay them $1 to make sure the walkway to our door was swept clean every week, free from trash, leaves, and bugs. Besides having a clean walkway for guests, this was a simple way to illustrate the importance of showing that we cared about how we maintained our home. As I told the boys: *Everything speaks!*

Of course, external appearances do not always show what is inside—that is why we have entertained angels unaware. Or, as we say, beauty is only skin deep. However, what you show on the outside should represent what is on the inside. Everything you do speaks of your values and your character. Your actions are the expression of who you are and what you believe. When you live in Spirit and truth, you live and love sincerely—from the center of who you are—and that will spill out as your witness.

Paul also makes it clear that love must be at the center of who we are and what we do. In 1 Corinthians 13, he says that even if we give away all we own to the poor, it means nothing if we do not have love.

How different this is from the Pharisees, who put up all kinds of external facades as a show. As Jesus said,

> "You clean the outside of the cup and dish, but inside they are full of greed and self-indulgence. Blind Pharisee! First clean the inside of the cup and dish, and then the outside also will be clean" (Matthew 23:25–26 NIV).

Leaders set an example in what they say and do: words and actions speak. Servant leaders set an example in how they serve: When we truly serve, the outside will always be an accurate representation of the inside. When we walk like Christ, with love and in the power of the Spirit, we will exhibit Christlike character to the world.

Make Your Mark

Pray about what it means to love sincerely from the center of who you are. Knowing that Christ is your center, commit to walk out your faith in Him by being a servant leader. If you respond to all things in life with the love of Jesus Christ, you will represent Him well.

Introducing

Kassie Dulin

Kassie is a politically savvy, modern-day freedom fighter. As communications director for First Liberty Institute, the largest law firm in the nation focused exclusively on defending religious freedom, Kassie is dedicated to standing up for biblical truth in the public arena. She helps her clients tell their story to the world through appearances in national media outlets like *The Kelly File, Good Morning America, CNN,* and *The Washington Post.* She also has a passion to see greater numbers of the evangelical community engaged in the political process and exercising their right to vote based upon biblical values. During the 2008 presidential campaign cycle, she served on Governor Mike Huckabee's campaign as the assistant to the national press secretary.

How do you hope to make a mark in the lives of others?

One of my greatest passions is standing up for biblical truth in the public arena and it has led me on some amazing adventures! I've testified before legislators at the United States Capitol about why we need religious freedom; I've stood on the steps of the Supreme Court and spoken in defense of marriage; I've organized press conferences for pastors who refused to hand over their sermons to the government; I've trained students at the Texas Capitol to be a voice for truth in government; and I've Marched for Life in Washington, DC. My prayer is that as people see me take a stand, they will be inspired to use their voice to defend biblical truth in the public arena.

How has your faith impacted your life?

My faith inspires everything I do. I fight for religious freedom so that people of faith can be free to serve God and advance His kingdom. On a more personal note, my faith has taught me that even if I'm fighting for the right things, but I don't have love, I am nothing. I pray that when people see me, they will be persuaded by my arguments, but won by my love. The work at First Liberty is challenging and demanding. It involves long hours, a crazy travel schedule, being on call 24/7, and coming under significant physical and spiritual attack, but it doesn't matter. What matters is my obedience and surrender motivated by my love for God.

Do you have a key mentor who has made a mark in your life?

The people who have made the greatest mark on my life are my parents, Steve and Melody Dulin. Throughout my life, I've seen their faith lead them to make tremendous sacrifices that few will ever see, from giving away all their finances to selling their company to go into ministry. No matter what God tells them to do, they will do it. Because of their example, I gave my life to Jesus at an early age and have followed Him ever since.

Do you have a guiding phrase you live by?

Do justly. Love mercy. Walk humbly with your God.

—Micah 6:8

Fun Facts About Kassie

- She enjoys rock climbing, cooking, and country music.
- She loves to travel. (This is good news, since she made over 30 trips last year alone.)
- She ran the Vote Under God Initiative for every election from 2008–2016

Introducing

Wendy K. Walters

Wendy is an entrepreneurial woman of integrity who is an expert in publishing, product development, and helping others create a signature brand identity. She has an enthusiastic and contagious gift to identify what makes a person unique, an ability to bring those things to the forefront, and the skill to maximize their originality. She is the author of *Marketing Your Mind, Selling Without Sleaze*, and *Intentionality—Live on Purpose*. She is also the founder of *The Favor Foundation*, a new philanthropic entity with a vision for planting businesses, creating income, and providing education here and in remote countries as a means of spreading the gospel. She was a worship leader for many years and today is an ordained minister, traveling and speaking at events all over the United States. She's at her very best when she is with her husband, Todd, and their three children.

How do you hope to make a mark in the lives of others?

I am most alive when I am helping other people articulate their passion and intentionally engage with God's highest and best for their lives. I speak life into what is dormant in others and help to nurture those things until they come into full expression. I believe the mark we make in others' lives is like our fingerprints left behind, proving where we have been and what we have touched. I desire that my fingerprints would be clear markers of my impact for good on the lives of others. When I help others excel in their calling, I know I've left an impression on their destiny that is God-honoring and life-giving.

How has your faith impacted your life?

I have served God all my days and, as a result, my faith shapes every aspect of my life. I grew up with no money but with lots of love and laughter. I have known success and failure, and like many others, have experienced betrayal, lack, and hardship. Through it all, He has delivered me from fear, disappointment, and trials. Therefore, I believe everything is possible and I deeply desire to ignite this faith-filled optimism in every person I encounter. No matter how far down they feel, no matter their lack of resources or connections, I believe that when they come into alignment with who God says they are and what He's called them to accomplish, the mountains of adversity and doubt will move or melt.

What advice would you give to another woman who is concerned about whether her life is impactful?

Whatever level of influence you feel you have, if you will become intentional with that influence, you will see an increase in its measure. You will see an increase in your impact. There is no such thing as a small life. When we are faithful with what (and whom) God has entrusted us, He multiplies our every action with His anointing and grace. God has equipped every person with special gifts and abilities. He has given each of us a one-of-a-kind personality, graced each of us with a distinct perspective, and fashioned each of us with His matchless grace. Your everyday life may feel narrow or small, but daily faithfulness in the small things produces tremendous impact in the big things.

Do you have a guiding phrase you live by?
Live with purpose, on purpose.

Fun Facts About Wendy
- She has been a worship leader for a black gospel choir in a mixed-race congregation.
- She loves Motown and blues.
- She plays the keyboard and writes songs.
- She is the seventh generation of a ministry family, but a first-generation entrepreneur.

Perhaps this is the moment for which you have been created.

—Mordecai to Esther in Esther 4:14

PART FOUR
Make Your Mark in Relationships

What's the most important thing people need? It's not money, achievement, or recognition. The most important thing people need is love. Love has the power to transform the human heart and bring us into a personal encounter with God.

First Corinthians 13 is one of the best-known and often-quoted chapters in the Bible. The apostle Paul spends the entire chapter defining love—not only what love is, or what it means, but also what it does, how it acts, and what its value is for every person. Paul says that love is greater even than faith and hope. And so, our human relationships are tightly interwoven with our relationship to God.

Our love relationship with God is a powerful catalyst for every other relationship in our lives. Through love we can connect in a way that brings health, joy, and hope to each other. It's love that connects and binds us together. It's love that builds long-term relationships and secures family legacies. It's love that heals. Love transforms relationships.

It is in and through relationships that we experience our greatest joys, navigate our most difficult experiences, and ultimately leave a lasting mark on others. That's why the quality of our relationships has such an enormous impact on all areas of our lives—in some sense, relationships are life. While not all of our relationships are going to be perfect or even healthy, we can respond in love to others in a way that reflects God's love for us.

The following devotions are focused on some of the most important areas of our relationships. Take some time to consider how well you are connecting with others. Then make a plan to invest more love in the most important relationships in your life or to develop some new ones.

Whether you are in a season of great trial or great joy, I pray that you will find wisdom and encouragement to walk well with others.

Day 25

Just Trust Me

Sandy Jobe

He makes my feet like the *feet of* a deer,

And sets me on my high places.

—Psalm 18:33 NKJV

One day while in Colorado, my husband and I decided to drive to the top of a mountain for a picnic. We started our ascent, which seemed to be straight up the mountain. I began to feel a little anxious and thought maybe we had made the wrong decision. Who cares about a picnic on top of a mountain anyway? The higher we went, the narrower the road became. One wrong move and it could have sent us plunging to our death.

As my husband was commenting on the beauty of the mountains and the tree lines, I was commenting, "Please keep your eyes on the road, and turn around as soon as there is an opportunity." He was determined to go all the way up and kept insisting that it would be worth it. "Trust me!" he said. I reluctantly agreed. After all, to turn around would only have put me closer to the road's edge.

Once we made it to the top, he was right. The scene was breathtaking. We could see for miles. There was a beautiful small lake on top of the mountain and we could see the small city down below. The treetops looked like they had been perfectly lined up. God is so creative.

This is what faith looks like. Proverbs 3:5 says to trust God with all your heart. Sometimes we can't see what is around the corner. Often, the path seems less traveled and the obstacles more than we want to encounter, but if we stay focused on the goal, the payoff can be amazing. If I had trusted my husband's judgment, that ride up the mountain would not have generated so much anxiety. We did get down the mountain safely; once back on lower ground, I was so grateful I had pressed through and that I didn't let the voice of fear keep me from experiencing such beauty. If you cannot see from God's perspective just yet, trust Him. Keep on climbing to the top through prayer. You will soon see things differently.

Make Your Mark

So often we must press through in faith and trust to get our breakthrough. What obstacles are in your way today? What are you believing God for? Just keep going. Trust Him and enjoy the journey. Great things are just around the bend—or up the mountain.

Day 26

The Struggle is Real

Adana Wilson

Two people are better off than one, for they can help
each other succeed. If one person falls, the other can
reach out and help. But someone who falls alone
is in real trouble.
—Ecclesiastes 4:9–10 NLT

L ife is full of struggles. The Bible says that God
is working in all things for our good, but it also
says that we are to glory in our sufferings. That
means every single one of us will struggle and go
through hard times. It doesn't matter what our
Facebook or Instagram pages say, how we look
on the outside, or how others perceive us—the
struggle is real.

One of the main goals of the enemy is to cause
us to struggle in isolation. John 10 gives an analogy

of a good shepherd who is God—how He loves, cares, and protects us. Jesus identifies Himself as the good shepherd. The good shepherd keeps the sheep together so that they can't be picked off and attacked by the wolf. The good shepherd knows that the sheep are safer when they stay together.

When we struggle alone, we will begin to believe the struggle will never change. But the truth is that struggles do pass, seasons do change, and there is nothing that you are walking through that you cannot overcome through Christ.

There was a secular study done years ago which showed that people who were connected in Christian community were more prosperous, more successful, and more fulfilled than those who weren't. Why is that? It is because we were created for community. We are not created to do life alone. We are not created to struggle in isolation. That is why God created the Church to be His Body.

When we stay connected in community and share our struggles, we realize that we are not alone, we hear the truth of God's Word, and we receive the support and encouragement we need.

Two verses later in Ecclesiastes, we read that
a strand of three cords is not easily broken. That
verse reminds us that there is one more aspect
of community: Our relationship with each other
is interwoven with our relationship with God.
Nothing can separate us from the love of God in
Christ Jesus (Romans 8:39).

Make Your Mark

Are you struggling today? Picture a strand of
three cords: you, a brother or sister in Christ, and
God. Are you connected in community? Take
a step today to engage in healthy community
through your church small groups or mentoring
ministry.

Day 27

Love Beyond

Hannah Etsebeth

Make every effort to live in peace with everyone and to
be holy; without holiness no one will see the Lord.
—Hebrews 12:14 NIV

B roken relationships are hard. From divorce to
estranged children, the aftermath of broken
relationships is often devastating and far-reaching.
The broken relationships I've witnessed between
parents and children have affected me the most.
It's heartbreaking when you see it, and it's even
worse when it happens to your family or among
your closest friends.

One thing I've learned as I've worked to sort out
my own heart is that I can't control other people's
actions. I can only control my own. I choose how I am
going to respond to a difficult or broken relationship.

I want to be someone who, like Jesus, can *love beyond*. I want to love beyond hurt. Love beyond betrayal. Love beyond a difference in opinion. Love beyond my pride. Love beyond *being right*. Let's choose to be humble enough to own our mistakes and forgiving enough to move forward in true forgiveness.

By choosing pure love, we acknowledge God's love toward us to a greater measure. He was betrayed more than you or I will ever experience. God forbid if I do not have grace for others in the same way that He has grace for me. I will never be one who walks away. I will stay and I will love beyond brokenness because of the grace He has shown me.

Make Your Mark

Are you struggling to love beyond hurt, disappointment, or pride? Take that relationship to God in prayer. Ask Him to fill you with His Spirit and change your heart toward the people and the relationship with which you are struggling. That is how you can experience holiness and share in His divine grace.

Day 28

Friendship

Dorothy Newton

A friend loves at all times, and a brother is born
for a time of adversity.
—Proverbs 17:17 NIV

The term friend can have quite a few meanings. Merriam-Webster says a friend is a person whom you like and enjoy being with or someone who helps or supports. Dictionary.com tells us that a friend is one person attached to another by feelings of affection or one who is on good terms with another. The Urban Dictionary is a bit more creative: Friends are people who are aware of how weird you are and still manage to be seen in public with you … or someone who knows all your Internet passwords.

Clearly, friends are different things to different people.

So what is the basis of friendship? I believe it is commonality. There must be something shared between two people as a reason to connect at all. Those connections can be established at work, school, or through other activities. That doesn't mean we should look or be the same; we just recognize a reason to share life. When we think of making new friendships, we often focus mostly on what the other person has to offer. Perhaps the key to friendship, however, lies in what we bring to the table.

Here are a few questions that are helpful in identifying what kind of friend we can be to others. They can help us understand what to expect from a friend, and, by extension, from our community.

- *How much time do you have to offer a new friend?*
  Building relationships of any kind requires time more than anything else. How much time will you be able to devote to a friendship? It is important for each person to know their expectations and limitations.

- *Do you recognize friendship as a give-and-take relationship?*

  Storybook, fairytale friendships rarely last. Inevitably, somebody will have a bad day, miss a date, or forget a birthday. The real question is how readily can we forgive and forget these instances. Recognizing the inevitable imperfection of human friendship helps us to remain in friendships for the long term.

- *How do you define the term best friend?*

  Many people think of a best friend as the person that will meet all their needs. This can create unrealistic expectations. No one person can be everything to anyone. It's best to understand how a friend fits into our overall community. A *best friendship* will likely develop on its own over time.

- *Are you willing to listen and learn?*

  A friend can be a sounding board for us to share our concerns and stories. However, it is selfish if it is all about you. God may have placed that person in your life to teach you something. Healthy friendships allow for both speaking and listening.

- *Are you able to remain non-judgmental, even if your friend tells you something that surprises you?*

How much and what kind of information we share depends on how safe we feel with the other person. If you appear warm and open, you may hear more about a person than you expect. Make it clear to your new friend that you will handle any and all information respectfully.

Make Your Mark

Do you want to be a better friend to others? Or are you just looking for a few new friends? Take a moment to ask yourself the questions above and then set about actively reaching out to others. Friendships are such an important part of our lives. Do everything you can to make the most of them.

Day 29

Me and My Gang

Adana Wilson

Let us think of ways to motivate one another
to acts of love and good works. And let us not neglect
our meeting together, as some people do,
but encourage one another, especially now
that the day of his return is drawing near.
—Hebrews 10:24–25 NLT

I have had many different seasons in my life. I
have been single and married; no kids and with
kids; worked full time and part-time. I have been
a stay-at-home mom and a working mom; I have
been just about everything except an empty-
nester, although I see that season on the horizon.
In every season, my desire has been to make my
mark—to make a difference in my home, church,
workplace, and community. The one constant in

every season is that I realize that I cannot make a difference alone.

Have you ever noticed there was no Lone Ranger in the Bible? When God called Moses to deliver the Israelites, He first sent Aaron to help him and then later sent Joshua. When God called Esther to help save her people, she had her uncle Mordecai to give her wisdom and counsel and help her fulfill her destiny. When Paul was commissioned to spread the gospel to the world, he was sent out with Barnabas. Even as Jesus fulfilled His ministry, He was surrounded by His disciples.

It is only in community that you fulfill God's destiny and plan for your life and truly make your mark. We need relationships with people in our lives who can support us, encourage us, challenge us, and mentor us.

Make Your Mark

What season of life are you in? Do you want to make your mark by raising great kids? Surround yourself with other moms who can encourage and mentor you. Do you want to make your mark in the marketplace? Seek out other women who are a little ahead of you in their careers and who you can walk alongside and learn from. Walking in community with other women in similar seasons will help you become what God has called you to be. We are created to do life together.

Day 30

Bear One Another's Burdens

Sandy Jobe

In my distress I called to the Lord; I cried to my God
for help. From his temple he heard my voice; my cry
came before him, into his ears. He brought me out into a
spacious place; he rescued me because he delighted in me.
—Psalm 18:6, 19 NIV

A couple of years ago while traveling in South
America, we came upon a farmer walking his
pack mule down the road. It was a hilarious scene.
The pack mule's load was twice as high and wide as
the poor animal. It reminded me of how some of us
carry loads way larger than our capacity.

Bearing someone else's burden is the natural
response to caring for those whom you love.
Bearing a burden is to identify with what someone
is actually feeling. Through empathy, you feel

some of the same emotions and carry some of the same weight. It is what Jesus did. The apostle Paul says that when we bear one another's burdens, we fulfill the law of Christ (Galatians 6:2). The law of Christ is love. When we bear or help carry someone else's burden, we exemplify Christ's love to them in the purest sense of the word.

When you love deeply, sometimes you carry burdens deeply. You can get weighed down by a heavy burden in your heart. However, you need not remain like that pack mule, weighed down so that you cannot function in any other way. At such a time, your burden bearing should be a trigger for intercession. If someone else's burden becomes a heavy burden to you, then you can pray and share that struggle with God—He will provide the strength that you need to carry it through. He shares the total weight with you and you can sense peace and release.

Jesus' death on the cross for our sins was the ultimate picture of Him carrying our burdens. He carried away all the burdens of the entire world. Some burdens bring with them a heavy weight of stressful emotion. However, when we share someone's distress with our heart, we can then respond to their need with love and compassion. This part of burden bearing actually brings healing.

Make Your Mark

What burdens of others are you carrying right now? Are they truly burdens God has asked you to share? Take some time today not only to tell the Lord about the burden, but also to tell Him how you feel. If it is a heavy burden, pray about it in the Spirit until you sense the peace of God increasing in your heart. Remember, Jesus has already borne all our burdens, and if we follow Him, our yoke will feel light.

Speak Up, Speak Out

Samantha Golden

Speak up for the people who have no voice, for the
rights of all the down-and-outers. Speak out for justice!
Stand up for the poor and destitute.
—Proverbs 31:8–9 MSG

When I was a little girl growing up in Graham, Texas, I wanted to be a mix of Mother Teresa and Princess Diana. I wanted to help the hurting and make a difference in the world.

I admired Mother Teresa and Princess Diana for their humanitarian work. Mother Teresa worked with the poorest of the poor in India, bringing them hope and dignity. Princess Diana would visit the terminally ill in hospices across the world to raise awareness of their diseases and show compassion for those who were suffering. Diana was once quoted as saying, "HIV does not make people dangerous to know. You can shake their hands and give them a hug. Heaven knows they need it." I respected that these two women were fearless in how they loved, that they saw the value in humanity, and they spent their lives making a difference.

My life didn't go exactly how I dreamed.

I gave birth to my first daughter at seventeen and had four beautiful daughters by the time I was twenty-four. I loved being a mom, but I still had a burning desire to help the hurting. At that stage of life, I thought I had little time or capacity to do anything to help others. So I asked the Lord to show me how I could serve and make a difference in my community, even amid raising my girls. He did just that.

To my surprise, God opened my eyes to three elderly ladies living on my street. Two of the women had just recently become widows and were adjusting to their new normal. My daughters and I started cooking dinner for them and would take food to each of them a couple of times a week. My girls would also go next door to Mrs. Hayes' house and keep her company by making her cards and coloring pictures for her. One year, we bought Christmas presents for the woman at the end of our street. My girls had so much fun serving our neighbors that they went back to their rooms to see what else they could find to give away. I found that I didn't have to go far to help and love on people.

We all learned valuable lessons from that experience: I learned that I could make a difference on my street as a stay-at-home mom and my daughters developed a heart for the people around them and learned to be givers.

Make Your Mark

Read Matthew 25:34–40. Each of us has influence and we can all make a difference in the world. You are all called to be the hands and feet of Jesus, but this may look different for each person. Ask the Lord what this looks like for you. Ask Him to open your eyes to those around you who need a touch, a smile, and hope. Ask Him how you can bless and serve them.

It's Better with Friends

Marsia Van Wormer

Commit everything you do to the Lord.
Trust him, and he will help you.
—Psalm 37:5 NLT

I was a very young 30 years old when my first child was born, and by the age of 35, I had our third and final little nugget. I basically spent my 30s pregnant and raising babies. I had left behind an intense executive position and most of my goals-driven friends who had chosen career over family.

For 10 years, I lived mostly sleep-deprived while I changed diapers and chased after little ones. I was a mom with personal goals and a crazy personal drive that allowed me to function in pressure situations without ever thinking about giving up. Yet, I would catch myself daydreaming about my life as an executive. I wasn't dreaming about my success as an executive, that part was becoming a very hazy memory. Yet, I found myself daydreaming about the previous season in my life because I missed the friendships I had made at work that had shaped me in many ways.

As I rocked my babies to sleep, I asked God to open the door for me to experience friendships even richer than I had before: the kind of friends I would have for a lifetime. I wanted God-given friends; friends who could help me smooth out the sharp corners of my life; who would embrace my larger-than-life personality; and for whom I could be a God-given friend in return.

When we wait on the Lord, for both the little and the big things, He rewards us with the best things. God only has the best to offer. The challenge is to wait for God's perfect timing.

Recently, while at dinner celebrating one of my best friend's birthday, I looked around at eight of the most life-giving, God-given friends I could ever have hoped for. I marveled at God's answer to my prayer and thanked Him for it. The friendships

I have now were worth the wait. God's timing is perfect.

Make Your Mark

Make a list of people you consider to be some of your best God-given friends. Carefully evaluate your list and add a short description of what each friend brings into your life (this friend makes me: fearless, laugh, take risks, etc.). Ask God to show you how He wants to use you to bless them in return. Thank God for who is in your life and pray for them.

Introducing

Edra Hughes

If you are at Gateway Church for very long, you will encounter the most extraordinary woman named Edra. Some have joked that she is the chief volunteer. She can be found at every major gathering and sometimes at the coffee bar. She's always greeting others and making them feel welcomed. Edra is a vibrant, faithful woman who is using her senior years to serve and bless others. After years of work in the marketplace, raising her two daughters, and the death of her wonderful husband of 46 years, Grady, she finds herself in one of the most impactful seasons of her life. She enjoys Bible study, volunteer work, and developing new friendships. She has a special impact on Gateway Church as the mother of Pastor Debbie Morris.

How do you hope to make a mark in the lives of others?

I don't always feel that I have any special impact or influence on others, but I can speak of my heart's desire. For many years, my desire has been to be an encourager, to speak positively into other's lives. I prayed that the Father would give me encouraging words to speak into the lives of hurting people. I pray for words that will help them see God's individual plans for them. I know that even in our darkest moments, we must see the light of Christ and realize His plan for us is peace, not for evil, to give us a future and a hope. When we walk in hope, it is easier to keep focused on the solution instead of the problem.

How has your faith impacted your life?

Faith is the foundation of my life. Over the years, I didn't think a lot about my faith in terms of its impact on others. I focused on my home, family, and work. I began my career at Mobil Petroleum in the data processing department. Eventually I became a wife and mother to two beautiful girls.

As my daughters were growing up, I was both a stay-at-home mom and a working mom. The girls grew up and became wives, and my grandchildren began to arrive. It wasn't until years later that I could see my faith was influencing those I love and cherish. Today, my children and grandchildren love the Lord, and all 25 of us attend church together and gladly serve in various ministries. Don't worry so much about impacting others; rather, focus on the assurance you have in your Heavenly Father who goes before you. Having that confidence will give you peace in knowing your faith has purpose and influence. Be obedient and trust the Lord to make your life impactful.

Do you have a key mentor who has made a mark in your life?

I am a living product of the prayers of my mother and mother-in-law.

Do you have a guiding phrase you live by?

Lord, don't let me get in the way of your plan.

Fun Facts About Edra

- She is grandmother to 11 grandchildren and 9 great-grandchildren.
- She got her gun license (CHL) along with five of her girlfriends.
- She learned to drive in a Model A Ford.

Introducing

Jessica Sheppard

Jessica is a style influencer, musician, lifestyle/portrait photographer, traveler, and an anything-is-possible dreamer. She currently serves as an associate worship pastor at Gateway Church, where she is the music director/pianist and travels with various music artists. When she's not playing music or taking pictures, Jessica is often pictured in front of the camera as a style blogger. She views her life as a story God is writing. Jessica opens the pages of her life on jessicasheppard.com, where she shares about faith, fashion, and fine art photography.

How do you hope to make a mark in the lives of others?

It has always been my desire to use whatever platform of influence I am given to be a positive influence on other people. I'm certainly not perfect, but I have surrendered my life to God's ways and do my best to honor Him in everything. I remember growing up admiring Rebecca St. James (Christian singer/songwriter/author), who was largely known for her openness about virginity. When I was about 11 years old, I attended a True Love Waits event she hosted and felt the Lord speak to me to save not only my body for my husband but also my heart. As a result, I chose to not consider dating relationships until I was at an age to consider marriage. Although this is a unique calling, God's grace is written on every page and I am keenly aware that He wants to write the story of His faithfulness through my life. This has become the most impactful decision in my entire life, next to asking Jesus to be my Lord and Savior. Even though Rebecca didn't have a direct effect on me at a personal level, she planted a seed by the way she shared her life through her platform of influence.

In the same way, you are making an impact on people observing your life—no matter how big the platform or social media following. In fact, you reach people that I cannot. You never know who you are influencing, so be an example in speech, in conduct, in love, in faith, and in purity (1 Timothy 4:12).

As the Lord continues to write the story of my own life, I hope it inspires other girls to set their standards high, make purity a priority, trust God in all things, give their talents to Him, and dream big, because He will do immeasurably more than we could ever ask or think! (Ephesians 3:20).

How has your faith impacted your life?

As a creative, I believe our ideas are God-breathed and God-inspired because we are created in the image of the ultimate Creator. That is why I believe the Church should be the most creative force in the world. We bring Him pleasure when we use our gifts to honor Him. This is true worship.

Do you have a key mentor who has made a mark in your life?

I'm blessed to be surrounded by many godly leaders. Each of them has left their fingerprints on my life in a unique way, but at the end of the day my parents top the list of those who have left a mark.

My dad has been in Christian music for longer than he'd be willing to admit. He is truly one of the men who paved the way for worship music as we know it today. He spotted my mom at one of his concerts, asked the pastor for her address, and started writing her letters. They were married within five months, and the rest is history.

One of the things I admire most about my parents is that they raised me to believe that with God's help I could do anything I set my heart and mind to. They never pushed me to follow in my dad's musical footsteps, but once I started taking classical piano lessons at the age of 5, they said quitting wasn't an option. I had rough days of not wanting to practice or wishing I could give up on lessons, but my parents saw a natural ability in me. Because of their influence, God's faithfulness met my diligence and multiplied my efforts. Their wisdom, encouragement, and guidance impacts my life every day. Mom's hotline-to-heaven prayers don't hurt either ... I need all the help I can get.

Do you have a guiding phrase you live by?

Grow gracefully, think eternally, pray courageously, lead boldly, respond wisely, wait well, and dream forever—day by day, present in every moment.

Fun Facts About Jessica

- She can nap anywhere—anytime. It's a gift.
- She's never received a traffic violation.
- She travels as often as possible. Just last year she stayed in a treehouse, a train caboose, an Airstream trailer, and a yurt.

Beautiful, you are capable
of amazing things.

PART FIVE
Make Your Mark
in the Kingdom

Throughout history, many women have been recognized as great heroes of the faith, accomplishing remarkable things in the name of Christ. Some of those women we know, but countless others have fought the fight, lived fully, and loved generously without human accolades or public appreciation. After all, our gauge for greatness is not fame or public reward. Our greatness begins with a heart of love and a lifetime of service. It's our ability to express our faith with compassion and love toward others that will determine the measure of our influence.

This kind of impact is most often developed in the private and unseen realm of the heart. Our ability to build, influence, or serve the kingdom of God begins with the position of our spirit. If we want to fully accomplish our purpose and honor God with our lives, then we must begin with the internal work of character development. It's in the intimacy of our personal relationship with Christ that our faith is developed, and it's in the response to His love that we will effectively serve others.

These final devotions are not focused on helping you develop a résumé of greatness, but rather they seek to draw your focus to the foundations of your faith. Do you trust God? Are you steadfast in waiting? Is your confidence and hope in Christ? Do you love with abandon and serve with passion? These are the issues that will determine your ability to leave a mark on others that is profound, eternal, and life-giving. It's your character that most beautifully reflects the mark of love left by a vibrant relationship with Christ.

You are called to be a difference maker. You are equipped to build the kingdom. You are able to make your mark.

Day 33

Strong and Free

Stephanie Kelsey

You may think you can condemn such people,
but you are just as bad, and you have no excuse!
When you say they are wicked and should be punished,
you are condemning yourself, for you who judge
others do these very same things.
—Romans 2:1 NLT

I walk a fine line. I feel it is important to hold strongly to my personal convictions, values, and beliefs. However, it is all too easy for me to turn those same convictions into judgment and condemnation of others. When I judge others by my standards, I may look strong, especially to those who agree with my way of thinking and acting. However, I also can fall short and risk being a hypocrite. I will inevitably lose my true freedom to comparison and condemnation.

God has opened my eyes to how He has different walks for different people. People can have different standards and beliefs and we all have different perspectives based upon our experiences. Nowhere does the Bible say that others need to see God through my lenses. It is good for me to remember that every person I meet has been brought up differently and has battles, past and present, that I know absolutely nothing about.

I really want both myself and others to walk strong and free. What does that look like? Strong is the ability to stand firm in my beliefs and convictions with humility, walking out with confidence the call that God has put on my life. Free is to live without the bondage of comparison, judgement, or control toward any other person. Strong and free looks like walking in my identity, purposes, passions, and love according to my relationship with Christ.

Strong and free looks like what the apostle Paul described:

For by the grace given me I say to every one of you: Do not think of yourself more highly than you ought, but rather think of yourself with sober judgment, in accordance with the faith God has distributed to each of you (Romans 12:3).

When I am strong and free, I am able to be all God created me to be while celebrating the differences and beauty in others. When others are strong and free as well, the kingdom of God thrives.

Make Your Mark

Where do you compare yourself to others? Are you strong, but not free? Are you free, but not strong? Pray that God will create in you a strong and free heart: one that sees others the way God sees them and that sees yourself the way that God sees you. Love yourself without pride and arrogance. God has given everyone different gifts and talents. Love others with the love and compassion of Christ and recognize the beauty of His handiwork in them.

Day 34

Can You Hear Me Now?

Jan Greenwood

Master, to whom would we go? You have the words
of real life, eternal life. We've already committed
ourselves, confident that you are the Holy One of God.
—John 6:68–69 MSG

T he book of John is full of miracles, healings,
and unusual experiences for many people
who crossed paths with Jesus. I noticed the
connection that Jesus kept pointing out between
hearing and believing.

Consider the Samaritan woman in John 4, who
heard and believed. She had every reason to roll
her eyes and walk away, but when He spoke, she
listened and believed.

In John 5, a man had been lying by the water of
the pool of Bethesda for 38 years. When Jesus asked

him, "Do you want to be healed?" the man answered with an explanation of why he couldn't be healed. Jesus looked straight at him and said, "Get up. Roll up your mat. Walk." The Bible says he was healed on the spot. Apparently, he listened and believed.

Look at the many followers and religious leaders to whom Jesus spoke in John 6 about His body and His blood. He went into a gory and visceral explanation about how they had to eat His body and drink His blood to enter into eternal life. The Scripture says that many turned away. Even His disciples said, "This is a tough teaching. Too hard to swallow." They heard, but they didn't believe.

Christ has said some hard things to me in the last year, things I found "hard to swallow." It's been difficult because the believing precedes the miracle. It can be hard because, though I hear, I have not yet seen.

I don't know if I would believe if I wasn't already fully committed and confident that Christ is the Holy One of God. Like Peter, I have already committed myself to Jesus and found that only He has the words of true life.

Therefore, I believe.

Let me encourage you to stretch your faith. In the Gospel of John, we can see how the ones who heard and believed experienced many miracles, healings, and supernatural signs and wonders.

The Samaritan woman became an evangelist, inviting a city full of people to come and meet a man who knew everything about her. When they arrived, they listened and believed as well.

The man at Bethesda didn't even know who helped him get healed. A few days later, he and Jesus crossed paths again in the temple, and he began to understand that the Messiah had come. He reported who healed him to the Jewish religious leaders. They listened and rejected him.

And what about the twelve disciples? Eleven listened and believed and changed the world. One listened but rejected Him and came to the end of himself.

Make Your Mark

Jesus is speaking to the whole world, but only a few are listening—even fewer can make the same confession as Simon Peter: only the Holy One of God has the words of life. If you face hardships you never expected, run straight to Jesus. Don't hold back. Ask Him to speak to you, then listen carefully. Listen again. Listen until hope springs up. It will be the sign that you believe. Then you will know: Miracles are coming.

Day 35

All in God's Time

Adana Wilson

There is a time for everything and a season for every
activity under the heavens.
—Ecclesiastes 3:1 NIV

Time. That simple four letter word means
so many different things to each of us.
Sometimes we wish we had more of it; we wish it
would slow it down or speed up; or we wish that we
could just get it to stand still.

We have all heard the phrase *timing is everything*. In cooking, the difference between a terrible
meal and a great meal is timing. In shopping, the
difference between a great deal and a steal is
timing.

The same could be said about the fulfillment of
our dreams. We all have dreams in our hearts that

we would love to see fulfilled, but we often do not see that one of the most important ingredients is timing: not our timing, but God's timing.

Several years ago, there was a class that I was excited about teaching. It was a dream of mine. The topic was near and dear to my heart and had made a huge impact in my life. I had made all the preparations, sent out invitations, and I was so excited to launch it. A few weeks before the class was to start, I was forced to stop and postpone it for another semester. I would love to say that my first response was godly, but it wasn't. I was more like a two-year-old throwing herself on the floor, kicking and screaming (at least on the inside that is what I was doing). I was so disappointed and frustrated. Several weeks into what would have been that class semester, however, events took place that would have caused me to stop the class if I had started it. It truly would have been a disaster. Praise God that I postponed that class!

God's timing is everything. If we will submit to His will, He will protect us, lead us, and fulfill the purposes He has for our lives.

As a side note, I was eventually able to start that class, and to this day, it remains one of my favorite things to do.

Make Your Mark

Are there some things in your life that you should surrender to God's timing? If so, pray about them and place them firmly in His hands; be willing to wait upon the Lord. You may need to talk to God about your disappointments or frustrations. In whatever situation you find yourself, remember that His timing is perfect. You can trust the Lord to fulfill your hopes, dreams, and promises at just the right moment.

Day 36

Let Go of Fear

Sandy Jobe

Fear not, for I *am* with you; be not dismayed, for I *am* your God. I will strengthen you, Yes, I will help you, I will uphold you with My righteous right hand.
—Isaiah 41:10 NKJV

For most of my life, I have struggled with fear. One summer, I decided I would conquer it once and for all. For vacation that year, we decided on a trip to Colorado. I suggested zip-lining for the entire family. My children, somewhat in disbelief, agreed to the adventure. (You see, I am not afraid of heights—just afraid of falling from those heights.) Only I secretly knew that my goal was to not be controlled another day by crippling fear.

As we donned the zip-lining gear and secured our helmets, my heart began to race. As I climbed several flights of stairs to get to the first platform, I could feel the oxygen required to breathe getting thinner and thinner. When I finally reached the top of the stairs, my legs felt like Jell-O. In fact, the instructor looked at me, handed me some water, and encouraged me to sit down and let the rest of our team go first.

They all reached the platform on the other side safely. It was now my turn. I actually was paralyzed by fear. The instructor said, "I will be right behind you—you can do this." Looking across to the next platform I could see all twenty people waiting for me to let go and glide through the sky. I had to coax myself the entire way. When I pushed off from the first platform, I kept my eyes closed and opened them right before it was time to make my landing. Another instructor, waiting for me on the other side, said, "You need to breathe!" Oh, yes! I had held my breath the entire time.

Little by little, platform to platform, the fear began to subside. By the time I made it to the tenth platform, I was flying through the air, hands free, eyes wide open, celebrating that I had conquered the fear. When we finished the tour, I thanked the instructor for helping and encouraging me. He said, "I could tell by the look on your face that you were going to bail and not make the tour. I didn't want you to miss out."

Make Your Mark

Are you gliding through life with your eyes closed and holding your breath, missing out on all the amazing things around you because you are afraid? What are you afraid of? The Maker of the universe is coaching you, encouraging you, and sustaining you in every aspect of your life. Don't bail when things get difficult. Let go of what you cannot control and let your Heavenly Father take you on the ride. Trust Him—it will be the best ride of your life.

Love in the Little Things

Marsia Van Wormer

Love other people as well as you do yourself.
You can't go wrong when you love others.
When you add up everything in the law code,
the sum total is *love*.
—Romans 13:10 MSG

I can't remember a time in my adult life when
someone has come to my house and I didn't
offer them something to eat or drink.

If a friend stops by to drop something off or
pick something up, I offer a bottle of water or a
random anything I have in my pantry. When the
pizza guy delivers, I always invite him in and offer
him something to drink before I pay him. When
my kids were small, we would wait for the garbage
truck to come around the corner and offer the men

working on them bottles of Gatorade. And cookies. Loving others is expressed in small acts of service.

Where did this desire come from to serve and welcome friends and strangers alike? One answer could be a mom who raised me with Emily Post as a guidebook, but I will add to this theory and say it came straight from the heart of heaven.

It's so simple really: Our responsibility as believers is to love everybody, always! It's love shown in the little things that forms a life that builds up and encourages others.

The moments serving friends who come by, the pizza guy standing in my entryway, or the garbage truck workers in the neighborhood may be brief, but the actions of love will echo in heaven: They are moments in time that help build the kingdom of God here on earth. As Jesus said, "Truly I tell you, whatever you did for one of the least of these brothers and sisters of mine, you did for me" (Matthew 25:40 NIV).

Make Your Mark

Make it a point for a week to track little things others do for you or small gestures you find out of the ordinary. Look for similar ways to serve others in your daily routine. Then practice that for a week and watch how God increases your love for others.

Day 38

What Do I Have to Offer?

Stephanie Kelsey

Brothers and sisters, God chose you to be his. Think about that! Not many of you were wise in the way the world judges wisdom. Not many of you had great influence, and not many of you came from important families. But God chose the foolish things of the world to shame the wise. He chose the weak things of the world to shame the strong. And God chose what the world thinks is not important—what the world hates and thinks is nothing. He chose these to destroy what the world thinks is important. God did this so that no one can stand before him and boast about anything.

—(1 Corinthians 1:26–29 ERV)

I was raised in Nebraska in a simple, loving family. With no real bells and whistles to speak of, I was never a big dreamer.

I suppose we were poor growing up; I remember times at the grocery checkout counter when my mom had me take items back to the shelf because we didn't have enough money for them. I never felt poor, because we had a loving family and a good life. Material things were never important to me: I was content with what I had and who I was, but I never understood what of real value I could offer to the world around me.

After getting married, I was a stay-at-home mom raising two kids, loving God, and loving my family. I knew that I loved God and His people with all my heart, but that didn't bring value when I was introduced to my husband's work associates and they asked that dreaded question, "What do you do?"

I found that answer in Scripture. One of my favorite things about God is how He would choose the most unlikely people to change the world. Gideon, Moses, David, Peter, and Esther are just a few examples of the most unlikely people God used in the Bible. They were just living their lives, loving God, and out of nowhere they encountered God and he gave them a world-changing role.

My life's mission has become to serve Him in the small, mundane, and ordinary places, with a strength of character and a passion for Jesus, so that if my Lord would ever need to call on me for any role—large or small—my heart would leap and shout, "Yes, Lord: Here I am, send me!"

Your significance does not come from a title, from what you do, or what you might do; your significance comes from being accepted by and connected to the Holy One, and serving Him in whatever way His Spirit leads you.

Make Your Mark

Do you tend to minimize your contribution to the world? Ask God, "What do I have to offer?" and journal His response to you. Listen to the Spirit daily and act when He shows you opportunities for service.

Day 39

The Faithfulness of God

Lynda Grove

I will declare the decree the Lord has said to me.
—Psalm 2:7 NKJV

My friend arrived in China overwhelmed with excitement and eager to explore the beauty and culture of the country. Her host escorted her to a beautiful hotel in a bustling area of the city. She had a reservation there because she was traveling alone and was assured of its safety and comfort for tourists. As she tried to check in, she was told the hotel was completely full—there was no room for her. Her host quickly assured her that she would be taken to another hotel.

When they arrived, she immediately knew she could not stay there. The hotel was in terrible shape and situated in an unsafe neighborhood. She refused to be left there and demanded the host take her back to the hotel where her reservations had been made.

She persisted despite the objections of her host. When she arrived, she demanded the hotel staff do whatever they had to do to make room for her. They actually made someone else leave so they would have room for her as the reservation promised.

When I heard her story, I was amazed that she had demanded her reservation be fulfilled—and that they did it!

Her courage made me wonder about my own. How many "missed" blessings had I walked away from because I surrendered to the limitations of the circumstances? How often has God made room for me, but I've surrendered my position, place, or influence because of circumstances or pressure?

David said that if we commit to God, we will be blessed. Like my traveler friend, King David had a bold courage that came from his knowledge of God's faithfulness to perform whatever He had promised.

Make Your Mark

God is always faithful to fulfill His promises. Whatever you face today, thank God for His faithfulness and boldly stand and wait for Him to *make room* for you.

Day 40

A Heart at Peace

Jan Greenwood

A heart at peace gives life to the body.
—Proverbs 14:30 NIV

The Lord has asked me to rest amid great turmoil and a life-threatening illness.

When God first asked me to rest, I could only imagine that He was asking me to do less, to cease activity. I soon discovered that no amount of sitting down brought me the kind of rest mandated by the Lord. Rather, He was asking me to go to a whole new level of trust, to really rest and place in His care everything that concerned me. He wanted me to experience peace.

Maybe you are like me, facing some significant challenges that are bigger than your ability to *work* your way out of them. If so, I hope the following three things I learned about pursuing peace will be a blessing to you:

1. *The body needs rest, but the mind needs truth.*
    I quickly realized that no amount of sleep was going to give me long-term peace. I could wake in the morning following a good night's rest and find my heart in my throat, filled with anxiety and fear. The key to sustainable rest, the kind that heals the body and the soul, is to treat the mind with truth. Truth drives out fear and helps brings peace.

2. *A heart at peace gives life to the body.*
    There is something miraculous about the body's healing power. When it is aligned with the will of God, it heals. This is true of a broken bone and a broken heart. When we come into agreement with the will and Word of God, there is a supernatural release that produces a natural blessing. Daily, set your heart in alignment with God, so that it may rest. This rest will produce a spring of peace.

3. *While we rest at peace, God works.*

I have perceived rest as wasted time. This has been a form of judgment against myself and others. Learning that our lack of productivity does not decrease our value in the eyes of God has been a game changer. When we can do nothing, God still works on our behalf. His favor and love are not a reward reserved for good performance, but rather a gift that constantly blesses our lives.

Make Your Mark

Take a moment to examine your own heart. Are you able to rest? Is there something within you that strives to take care of yourself or even to earn God's peace? Simply repent and invite God to activate His Word in your life so significantly that it becomes truth to you. Observe God's principle of Sabbath and receive the flood of healing and redemption that He has promised.

Introducing

Hala Saad

Hala was born and raised in Egypt in a loving Christian family. She migrated to the United States over thirty years ago. After years of working in the marketing and advertising arena, she became the founder and CEO of *Vision Communications*, a multimedia ministry in the Middle East that produces Arabic Christian television programming, films, social media outreaches, internet radio, and evangelistic rallies. She is also the founder of *Global Bounty*, a humanitarian organization that empowers and educates the poorest of Egypt's women, especially those who are sole providers for their families. She and her husband, Greg, split their time between their homes in Fort Worth and Cairo.

How do you hope to make a mark in the lives of others?

Our Lord is a God of restoration and healing. Over the years, He restored me spiritually, mentally, and emotionally and has allowed me to give out what I have freely and generously received to the people I reach through both the media ministry and the humanitarian programs. He also blessed me with a wonderful husband who has fully supported the call on my life.

How has your faith impacted your ability to influence others?

My love for the Lord and my personal faith walk are everything. What I do is simply a byproduct of my personal relationship with Christ. My identity is in Him, not in my career or ministry, or even my perceived influence. Being secure and joyous in my identity has been central to my ability and desire to influence others, whether through the television programs I've presented, the classes I've taught, the business counsel I've given, or in any one-on-one ministry opportunity. Even though I run a couple of organizations focused on reaching large numbers of people at once (what some would call outreach to the masses), I believe my greatest impact has been through investing in individuals through mentoring, prayer, instruction, and just being a trusted friend. I hope my personal story—my successes and my failures—can inspire and motivate others to embrace the call of God on their lives and to rise above their circumstances to be agents of change in their families, communities, and even the world.

What advice would you give to another woman who is concerned about whether her life is impactful?

Rest assured—be at rest and be assured—that God will see to it that you are a woman of real influence. I never set out to do great things. The culture I grew up in didn't encourage or teach women to be achievers, let alone leaders of others. On top of that, I made many mistakes and wandered away from God for years. But the moment I yielded to the Holy Spirit, He stepped in and led me toward my destiny. He sovereignly opened the doors. He made the divine connections. He released the anointing. He redeemed the time. And He paved the way for impact and exponential growth. You are always on a journey of preparation and training for what God has next. If nothing looks like it's happening, embrace this season as one of getting ready. Celebrate small beginnings as they unfold. Serve in any capacity you can and don't wait for the perfect opportunity. God will multiply every work.

Do you have a guiding phrase you live by?
Be kingdom-minded in everything you do.

Fun Facts About Hala
- She says being a part of a passionate and visionary church has been key to her success.
- She is naturally shy and has had to work hard to break out of her introverted shell.

Introducing

Amie Stockstill

Amie is a "top gun" of her generation, an impactful and engaging young leader who has a knack for making others feel seen and valued. She and her husband, Joel, travel around the nation teaching the Word of God and encouraging others to live a radical life of faith. Amie is a natural mentor and is gifted at creating confidence, building content for aspiring female leaders including *Echo*, a preaching seminar focused on preparing women to become transformative communicators. Whether they are at home in Dallas or in West Palm Beach, Amie enjoys producing content that reaches women all over the world.

How do you hope to make a mark in the lives of others?

When I got married in 2010, I hit a whirlwind of suffering, endless tears, and questioning God. My husband, Joel, has battled kidney failure for many years. Before my marriage, suffering had no part in my life experience. I was like a little bee, buzzing around with a great childhood, quality friends, and loving parents. Joel and his struggles helped awaken a deep level of faith in my heart so that I might be better equipped to love and serve others. God has used our struggles and worked through an intense brokenness in my life to shape me in ways I would not trade for the world. I have a special compassion for women who have walked through suffering of their own. It helps me relate to their difficulties and releases a genuine compassion for their pain. My prayer is that my life story will encourage others to continue the fight of faith despite great difficulties.

How has your faith impacted your life?

As a young girl, I knew the hand of God was on my life, but I did not know what to do about it. In 2006, I put a degree in interior design on hold and instead did an internship at my church, which stretched me to the limit. This experience established a strong foundation for my faith and set the course for my life in a totally new direction. It was during this internship that I first began mentoring at-risk youth and developing leadership gifts in others. Eventually, I decided to give my life to investing in others. Today, Joel and I have a God-given assignment to travel around the nation teaching at churches and conferences. I am committed to investing in others by stepping out of my comfort zone and communicating the Word of God with authenticity and power.

What advice would you give to another who is concerned about whether her life is impactful?

Your influence is already greater than you realize, but if you want your impact to increase then maximize each season by using your gifts to serve others. If you are a mom, influence other moms and give them a break by watching their kids. If you are single, encourage other singles to do all they can for God before they get married. If you are a student, offer to study with someone. If you aren't a student, offer to cook for one. If you are in the marketplace, bring the light of Jesus with boldness by working with joy and integrity. If you are a wife who is limited because of your husband's health, make some videos, write a blog, or speak life over your friends. Do something, do anything, and watch God breathe on it.

Do you have a guiding phrase you live by?

If you are not willing to learn, no one can help you.
If you are determined to learn, no one can stop you!
                                                —Zig Ziglar

Fun Facts About Amie

- She has a twin sister who is an adventure photographer and travels all over the world.

- She has a degree in interior design and a master's in practical theology.
- She loves adventure and wants to conquer all her fears.
- She is not a coffee lover. (Don't hate her.)

GATEWAY WOMEN

About Gateway Women

Gateway Women is led by Debbie Morris. She is the visionary leader behind Pink Impact and serves as the executive pastor of Gateway Women at Gateway Church. She is the author of *The Blessed Woman*, coauthor of *The Blessed Marriage* and *Living Right Side Up*, as well as editor-in-chief of *Studio G*, a magazine for women. She is a quiet but powerful influence in the lives of the women at Gateway Church, as well as the Christian community. Debbie's heart is to help women understand who they are in God, discover their destinies, and experience victory in life. As a wife who witnessed God turn her marriage around, she delights in encouraging women to believe God can and will do the same for them. Debbie is married to Pastor Robert Morris, her high school sweetheart and founding senior pastor of Gateway Church. They have been married for 36 years and have three married children and eight grandchildren.

About Pink Impact

Founded in 2006, Pink Impact is Gateway Church's annual conference for women. Pink Impact is renowned for providing women an opportunity to participate in an environment that exposes them to the goodness of God, invites them to join in His kingdom work, and saturates them in an empowering culture that celebrates women. Each year, thousands of women from around the world gather to engage in extravagant worship, be inspired by gifted communicators, and build new friendships.

Additional Resources
from Gateway Women

The Blessed Woman
Debbie Morris

Living Rightside Up
Debbie Morris and Friends

The Blessed Marriage
Debbie Morris

Women at War
Jan Greenwood

Gateway Worship Voices: Women of Gateway

Resources are available at store.gatewaypeople.com and Amazon.com